Oracle E-Business Suite 12.1

Payables Essentials

By

S Kaur & JK Hall

Copyright Notice

Table of Contents

Before you Start..

Before you start here are some Key features of the Oracle Payables Certification Exam.

➢ The Oracle E-Business Suite 12 Supply Chain Certified Implementation Specialist: **Oracle Payables** certification indicates a functional foundation in E-Business Essentials including skills such as how to access and navigate within the R12 E-Business Suite, how to enter data, retrieve information in the form of a query and access online help.

➢ Candidates must also demonstrate knowledge of Procure-to-Pay process flow, Payables process flow, Multiple Organization Access Controls (MOAC), Suppliers, Invoices, Payments, Expense Reports and Credit Cards, Period Close, Transaction Taxes in Payables, Withholding Tax and Advances and Progressive Contract Financing.

➢ The exam is Computer based and you have 150 minutes to answer 80 Questions.

➢ The Questions are (mostly) multiple choice type and there is NO penalty for an incorrect answer.

➢ You are not allowed to use any reference materials during the certification test (no access to online documentation or to any system).

➢ The Official Pass percentage is 60%. (This can vary slightly for your exam)

➢ There are two sections to this exam, **E-business Essentials** & **Payables**. Both sections of the exam MUST be passed in order the pass the exam.

➢ In this book, unless otherwise stated, there is only one correct answer.

A Quick Quiz

Q1. With reference to Invoice Validation and Invoice Approval, which of the following statements are FALSE?

a. Invoices may be submitted for validation in one of the following three ways; System, Online or Batch

b. Approval rules can be Line-Level or Document-Level or both

c. Invoice Approval Workflow may be based on the total Invoice value

d. If an approver rejects an invoice, then you cannot use the Force Approval option to manually approve the invoice

Answer; d

Explanation;

Process for Invoice Validation

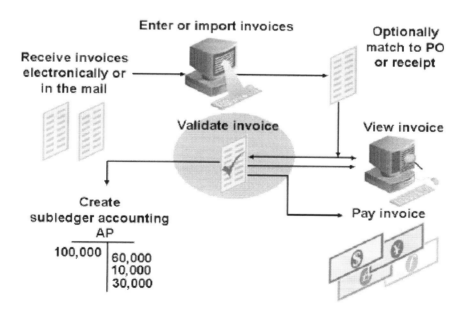

There are three Levels of Invoice Validation;

System level validation

Manually submit the Payables Invoice Validation process or schedule it to run periodically from the Submit Request window. Submit the Payables Invoice Validation process right before you process payments to update the status on all invoices. Payables will use the Option parameter to select unvalidated invoices for validation. Enter All to ensure you release any existing holds on invoices as well as place new holds. Otherwise, Invoice Validation reviews only those invoice distributions that were not already reviewed by Invoice Validation. Optionally, enter other criteria to submit Invoice Validation for specific groups of invoices.

Batch level validation

Submit Invoice Validation for one or more invoice batches from the Invoice Batches window. Batch level validation is only allowed if the Allow online validation Payables option is enabled also.

Invoice level (online) validation

If the Payables option to allow online validation is enabled, you can submit online validation for one or more individual invoices when an invoice must be validated and paid immediately. You can also validate related invoices for credit and debit memos by choosing Validate Related Invoices in the Actions window after you enter a credit or debit memo.

Invoice Approval Levels

The Invoice Approval Workflow process uses Oracle Approvals Management and Oracle Workflow to enable you to define business rules to determine who approves invoices and how they will be routed for approval to different approvers

Approving Invoices at the Line Level

Line-level approval is the approval of one specific line or set of lines within an invoice, rather than approving the entire document. Approvers have access to the Notification Detail and

Interactive Line Details pages to review the invoice details. The pages display only the appropriate level of information for the approver to view. That is, approvers view only the information that they can approve or reject. Furthermore, no additional login or privileges are required for the approver to approve. The self-service login that an approver uses to view the notifications is sufficient to review the invoice information.

Approving Invoices at the Document (Invoice) Level

Review the invoice and approve it, as necessary. If line-level approval is enabled, review the invoice line information before you approve or reject the entire invoice.

Invoice Approval Workflow

The workflow then sequentially asks each approver in the approval list to approve invoices online. For example, you can define a rule so invoices over $100,000 require CFO approval and then CEO approval.

Notification from Approvers

Approvers can approve or reject the invoice.

• If an approver approves the invoice, then the invoice goes to the next person in the approver list until all required people approve the invoice.

•If an approver rejects an invoice, then you can perform one of the following actions from the Invoice Actions window:

>   • *Use the Force Approval option to manually approve the invoice*

>   • Use the Initiate Approval option to resubmit the invoice to the Invoice Approval Workflow
>   after correcting any issue that caused the approver to reject the invoice

>   • Use the Cancel Invoice option to cancel the invoice

Q2. Which of the following types of 'adjustment invoices' are supported by Oracle Payables?

a. Minor Adjustment Invoice

b. Item Adjustment Invoice

c. Purchase Order Price adjustment Invoice

d. Sales Order adjustment Invoice

Answer; c

Explanation;

The **two** types of adjustment invoices supported are:

PO Price Adjustment Invoice

This invoice is for the difference in price between the original invoice and the new purchase

order price. PO price adjustment invoices can be matched to both purchase orders and invoices.

Adjustment Invoice

This invoice effectively reverses any outstanding regular Payables price corrections and PO

Price Adjustment invoices. This is so the PO Price Adjustment document can be for only the

price difference between the original invoice and the new PO price.

These adjustment invoices can be positive, negative, or zero amount. When the original

invoice and its related adjustment documents are paid, the net effect is as if the original

invoice had always had the new price. The supplier is paid the appropriate amount, and the

accounting is adjusted accordingly.

You cannot manually enter these types of invoices, nor can you adjust or cancel them. You

can view, report on, validate, account for, and pay them.

Q3. Which of the following options can influence the assignment of a default GL date for an Invoice?

*(**Note:** More than one answer may be correct)*

a. Receipt/Invoice

b. System Date

c. Period closing date

d. Receipt/System

Answer; a, b, d

Explanation;

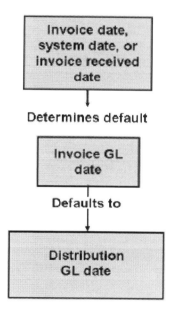

The figure above shows how the default GL date is assigned.

Payables determines the accounting period in which an invoice or payment is included by

comparing the invoice or payment GL date to the ranges of dates you have defined for your

accounting periods in your accounting calendar. The default invoice GL date is based on the

GL Date Basis Payables option. Payables automatically defaults this GL date to new invoice

distributions added to the invoice. If you specify a GL date on the invoice batch, that GL date defaults to invoices you enter into the batch. You can change the GL date for individual

invoice lines. The GL date is stored at the invoice header so if you were to add additional

invoice lines, the GL dates on the lines would be the same as the date on the invoice header.

The GL Date Basis Payables option determines what date is used as the GL date. The GL

date for each invoice defaults based on one of the following options:

• **Invoice date**

• **System date**

• **Receipt/Invoice**

• **Receipt/System**

(Payables uses the payment date as the GL date for your payments.)

Q4. In an Invoice, Distribution details include invoice accounting details, the GL date, charge accounts etc. An invoice line can have one or more invoice distributions.

Invoice distributions can be created on an invoice in a variety of different ways.

Which of the following is NOT a valid way to create Invoice distribution?

a. Manual

b. Distribution Set

c. Adjustment

d. Allocation

Answer: c

Explanation;

The following figure shows the different ways to enter distributions.

Manual Entry

Click the Distributions button to manually add the distributions to the invoice.

Distribution Set

Specify a distribution set for the invoice. A distribution set is a template for invoice distributions. When you specify a distribution set for an invoice, Payables automatically creates invoice distributions based on the distribution set.

Full Distribution Sets

Use Full Distribution Sets to create distributions with set percentage amounts, or use Skeleton Distribution Sets to create distributions with no set distribution amounts. For example, a Full Distribution Set for a rent invoice assigns 70% of the invoice amount to the Sales facility expense account and 30% to the Administration facility expense account.

Skeleton Distribution Sets

A Skeleton Distribution Set for the same invoice would create one distribution for the Sales facility expense account and one distribution for the Administration facility expense account, leaving the amounts zero. You could then enter amounts during invoice entry depending on variables such as that month's headcount for each group.

If you enable and use a descriptive flexfield with your distribution set lines, the data in the flexfield will be copied to the invoice distributions created by the Distribution Set.

Matching

Match the invoice to a purchase order or receipt and creates invoice distributions.

Invoice Validation

If you are using automatic withholding tax or automatic tax calculation, the Validation process can automatically create the necessary tax distributions.

Allocation

Use the Allocation window to create freight and miscellaneous distributions. Individual freight distributions can be added by specifying the distribution amounts.

Q5. Which of the following statements are FALSE regarding 'Quick Invoices'?

a. You use 'Quick Invoices' functionality for rapid, high–volume entry of Standard and Credit Memo invoices that are not complex and do not require extensive online validation.

b. The invoice records you enter in the Quick Invoices window are stored in interface tables: AP_INVOICES_INTERFACE and AP_INVOICE_LINES_INTERFACE.

c. If you have successfully imported an invoice record and want to modify it, you can use the Quick Invoice Window for the modification.

d. Quick Invoices Batch name may be used to query the group of invoice records in the Quick Invoices window.

Answer; c

Explanation;

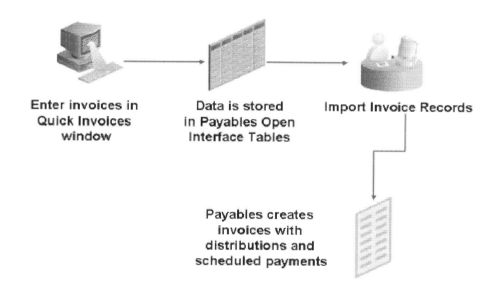

Enter invoices in
Quick Invoices
window

Data is stored
in Payables Open
Interface Tables

Import Invoice Records

Payables creates
invoices with
distributions and
scheduled payments

The picture above describes the quick invoices process.

You use the Quick Invoices window for your everyday entry of invoice records. You use this

window for rapid, high–volume entry of Standard and Credit Memo invoices that are not

complex and do not require extensive online validation or defaulting of values during entry.

You can use this window for purchase order matching and for applying prepayments to the invoice you are entering.

The information entered in the Quick Invoices window is stored in the Payables Open Interface tables. Because the system performs limited validation and defaulting of invoice values while you are entering invoices, you can enter invoices more quickly in the Quick Invoices window than you can in the Invoice Workbench.

When you enter invoice records in the Quick Invoices window, you can submit a customized workflow program to automate your processes for managing invoices. For example, you can customize the workflow program to validate the cost center on all invoices before you import them.

The invoice records you enter in the Quick Invoices window are stored in interface tables: AP_INVOICES_INTERFACE and AP_INVOICE_LINES_INTERFACE.

These tables store invoice header and line information.

Import invoice records by using the Create Invoices window, or by submitting the Payables Open Interface Import Program from the Submit Request window.

Payables validates the invoice records during import and creates invoices with distributions and scheduled payments.

You can use the Quick Invoices Batch name to query the group of invoice records in the Quick Invoices window, and to identify a group of invoice records that you want to import together.

Note that if you use invoice batch control and you want to maintain the grouping of invoices after import, then when you submit import for the Quick Invoices batch, you can assign an Invoice Batch name to the group of invoices that Payables creates.

You can then use the Invoice Batch name to query the same group of invoices in the Invoice Workbench.

If you have successfully imported an invoice record and want to modify it, you must use the Invoice Workbench.

If you have NOT imported an invoice record and want to modify it, you can use the Quick Invoice Window.

When correcting problems with invoice records rejected during import, you can find the rejection reason by looking at the Payables Open Interface Import Report, or you can query the record in the Quick Invoices window and choose the Rejections button to see the rejection reason in the Rejections window.

ORACLE ACCOUNTS PAYABLE

1. **This module is a high-productivity accounting solution that helps you maintain strong financial controls in maximizing supplier discounts, preventing duplicate payments and pay for only goods and services that has been received. What do you call this Oracle module?**

   a. Oracle iReceivables
   b. Oracle General Ledger
   c. Oracle Payables
   d. Oracle iPayments

   Answer: c

   Explanation:

   Oracle Payables is a high-productivity accounting solution that helps you maintain strong financial controls in maximizing supplier discounts, preventing duplicate payments and pay for only goods and services that has been received.

   Oracle iReceivables is an Internet-based, self-service application that both your customers and employees can use to access Receivables data. Oracle iReceivables provides personalized, secure access to online information using a standard web browser. Oracle iReceivables helps reduce the cost of billing and collections.

   Oracle General Ledger is a comprehensive financial management solution that dramatically enhances financial controls, data collection, information access, and financial reporting throughout your enterprise. Oracle General Ledger is part of Oracle Applications, an integrated suite of business solutions designed to support continuous process improvement for enterprises competing in time-critical markets.

   Oracle iPayment provides an integrated electronic payment solution for both electronic commerce applications and client-server applications. It provides integrated, user friendly access, and control of payment processing to these applications.

2. **Which of the following is not part of Oracle Payables major business functions?**

   a. Supplier entry
   b. Invoice import and or entry
   c. Invoice validation
   d. Sales Invoice

   Answer: d

   Explanation:

   Oracle Payables five major business functions:

   1) Supplier entry
   2) Invoice import and or entry
   3) Invoice validation
   4) Invoice payment

5) Invoice and payment accounting

3. **Which of the following is not use as an open interface to import data into Payables from other application or third party solutions?**

   a. Payables Open Interface
   b. Payables Expense Report Open Interface
   c. Payables PCard Open Interface
   d. AR_PAYMENTS_INTERFACE_ALL

   Answer: d

   Explanation:

   Use the following open interfaces to import data into Payables from other applications or third party Solutions:

   1) Payables Open Interface
   2) Payables Expense Report Open Interface
   3) Payables PCard Open Interface
   4) Payables Credit Card Open Interface
   5) Payables Matching Open Interface
   6) Payables Supplier Open Interface

   AR_PAYMENTS_INTERFACE_ALL is an interface table for payment receipts that needs to be populated via custom program for Autolockbox. This interface table is used for importing data from the data file provided by Bank.

4. **If activated, this workflow sends notifications to managers to approve employee procurement card transactions. What do you call this Payables Integration Workflow?**

   a. Credit Card Workflow
   b. Procurement Card Manager Approval Transaction Workflow
   c. Invoice Approval Workflow
   d. Procurement Card Employee Verification workflow

   Answer: b

   Explanation:

   Procurement Card Manager Approval Transaction Workflow - If activated, this workflow sends notifications to managers to approve employee procurement card transactions.

   Credit Card workflow - The Credit Card Transaction Manager Workflow is a predefined workflow that you can initiate to notify managers of transactions incurred by their direct reports. The Credit Card Transaction Manager Workflow determines if workflow will notify a manager of transactions created by the manager's employee's credit card, and it determines if the manager must approve the transactions.

   Invoice Approval Workflow - The Invoice Approval Workflow automates your invoice approval process. Based on rules you define, the workflow determines if an invoice or invoice line needs approval, who the approvers are, and in what order approvers should approve payment of the invoice.

Procurement Card Employee Verification workflow - If activated, this workflow sends notifications to employees related to their procurement card transactions. Depending on how the procurement cards are set up, the employee may be required to verify expenditures.

5. **It is an open interface used to load invoices from a variety of sources including invoices generated from the Pay on Receipt Autoinvoice process, EDI invoices generated by the e-Commerce Gateway, invoices from credit card and procurement card transactions and invoices from external systems. What do you call this open interface?**

    a. Payables Invoice Open Interface
    b. Payables PCard Open Interface
    c. Payables Credit Card Open Interface
    d. Payables Supplier Open Interface

    Answer: a

    Explanation:

    Payable Invoice Open Interface is an open interface used to load invoices from a variety of sources including invoices generated from the Pay on Receipt Autoinvoice process, EDI invoices generated by the e-Commerce Gateway, invoices from credit card and procurement card transactions and invoices from external systems.

    Payables PCard Open Interface is used to streamline your procure-to-pay process by implementing a procurement card program. Employees purchase items directly from suppliers using a credit card and then the credit card issuer sends transaction files directly to your company. You can import credit card transaction files from your card issuer directly into Payables helping you reduce transaction costs and eliminate low dollar value invoices.

    Payables Credit Card Open Interface uses SQL*Loader scripts to load credit card transactions for corporate credit (travel) cards into the open interface if you are using a credit card program. Corporate credit (travel) cards are similar to procurement cards but are generally used for travel expenses. After transactions are validated, you include them in expense reports you enter through the Self Service Web Applications.

    Payables Supplier Open Interface is used to load supplier data from external systems. You can load suppliers, supplier sites, and supplier contacts using this Open Interfaces.

6. **Which of the following Oracle application does not use Supplier Information?**

    a. Order Management
    b. Payables
    c. Purchasing
    d. Assets

    Answer: a

    Explanation:

    Oracle Applications that share supplier information are:

    1) Purchasing
    2) Payables
    3) Assets
    4) Property Manager
    5) Multiple Organization Access Control (MOAC)
    6) Trading Community Architecture
    7) iSupplier Portal

7. **Vendor Type, Minority Group, Pay Group Freight Terms, Ship_Via and FOB are called?**

    a. Payables Groupings
    b. Payable Options
    c. Payables Lookup Codes
    d. Financial Options

    Answer: c

    Explanation:

    Payables Lookup Codes are:

    1) Vendor/Supplier Type
    2) Minority Group
    3) Pay Group
    4) Freight Terms
    5) Ship_Via
    6) FOB

    Illustration:

Lookup Codes

VENDOR TYPE
MINORITY GROUP
PAY GROUP
FREIGHT TERMS
SHIP_VIA
FOB

8. **You can control supplier information using security, numbering, duplicate supplier entry, setup options (defaults) and _____. Which of the following is also used as control for Supplier Information?**

    a. Tax Defaults
    b. Invoice Number
    c. Purchase Order
    d. Approved Purchase Requisitions

Answer: a

Explanation:

Control supplier information using:

1) Security
2) Numbering
3) Duplicate supplier entry
4) Setup options (defaults)
5) Tax Defaults

9. **It is an Oracle Procure to Pay process that covers the business activities related to the search, qualification, and selection of suitable suppliers for requested goods and services. What do you call this Procure to Pay process?**

   a. Demand
   b. Source
   c. Order
   d. Receive

Answer: b

Explanation:

Oracle Procure to Pay Process

Demand - The procurement process generates and manages requests for the purchase of goods. The demand for purchase items may be a one-time event or may recur in either predictable or random time intervals.

Source - The procurement sourcing process covers the business activities related to the search, qualification, and selection of suitable suppliers for requested goods and services.

Order - The procurement ordering process includes purchase order placement by the buying organization and purchase order execution by the supplying organization.

Receive - The receipt process acknowledges that a purchase order has been duly executed. For orders of physical goods, it will typically include the receipt, inspection and delivery of the goods to inventory or to another designated location. For orders of services, it will typically consist of a notification from the requester or the approving person that the service has been performed as agreed.

Invoice - The invoice process includes entering supplier and employee invoices.

Pay - The payment process consists of those activities involved in the payment for ordered goods and services.

Illustration:

Oracle Procure to Pay Process

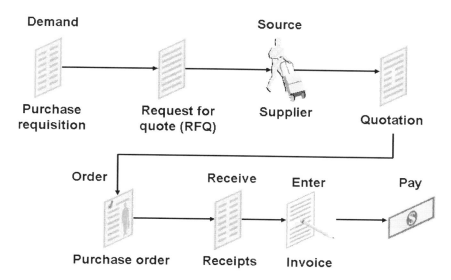

10. **Identify which statements that is not true about bank and supplier payment.**

    a.   Primary bank account can be only at the supplier site.
    b.   Supplier's payment requires a bank account with at least one payment document.
    c.   Use the Banking Details page to create bank accounts for making payments to suppliers.
    d.   If bank accounts for a supplier site are entered, Payables defaults the supplier's active bank accounts.

    Answer: a

    Explanation:

    Primary Bank Account can be assign for each supplier and supplier site that has bank account assignments. The primary bank account is used by Payables as a default when you pay this supplier electronically. You may override the default if necessary.

11. **It is a type of purchase orders where you know the detail of the goods or services you plan to buy from a specific supplier in a period, but you do not yet know the detail of your deliver schedule. What type of purchase order will you create?**

    a.   Standard Purchase Order
    b.   Blanket Purchase Agreement
    c.   Contract Purchase Agreement
    d.   Planned Order

    Answer: b

    Explanation:

    Purchasing supports four types of purchase orders:

    Standard: Create standard purchase orders for one-time purchases of various items. You create standard purchase orders when you know the details of the goods or services you require, estimated costs, quantities, delivery schedules, and accounting distributions. If you use encumbrance accounting, the purchase order may be encumbered since the required information is known.

Blanket: Create blanket purchase agreements when you know the detail of the goods or services you plan to buy from a specific supplier in a period, but you do not yet know the detail of your delivery schedules.

Contract: Create contract purchase agreements with your suppliers to agree on specific terms and conditions without indicating the goods and services that you will be purchasing.

Planned: A planned purchase order is a long-term agreement committing to buy items or services from a single source. You must specify tentative delivery schedules and all details for goods or services that you want to buy, including charge account, quantities, and estimated cost.

12. **This type of purchase order is commonly used for long-term agreement committing to buy items or services from a single source. You usually specify tentative delivery schedules and all details for goods or services that you want to buy, including charge account, quantities, and estimated cost. What type of Purchase Order is this?**

   a. Standard Purchase Order
   b. Blanket Purchase Agreement
   c. Contract Purchase Agreement
   d. Planned Order

   Answer: d

   Explanation:

   Purchasing supports four types of purchase orders:

   Standard: Create standard purchase orders for one-time purchases of various items. You create standard purchase orders when you know the details of the goods or services you require, estimated costs, quantities, delivery schedules, and accounting distributions. If you use encumbrance accounting, the purchase order may be encumbered since the required information is known.

   Blanket: Create blanket purchase agreements when you know the detail of the goods or services you plan to buy from a specific supplier in a period, but you do not yet know the detail of your delivery schedules.

   Contract: Create contract purchase agreements with your suppliers to agree on specific terms and conditions without indicating the goods and services that you will be purchasing.

   Planned: A planned purchase order is a long-term agreement committing to buy items or services from a single source. You must specify tentative delivery schedules and all details for goods or services that you want to buy, including charge account, quantities, and estimated cost.

13. **Oracle Payables integrates with Human Resources, Subledger Accounting, General Ledger, Workflow, Property Manager, Inventory, E-Business Tax and iExpense. Which of the following module also consider that has integration with Oracle Payables?**

   a. Order Management
   b. Alert
   c. MRP (Material Requirement Planning)
   d. Purchasing

   Answer: b

   Explanation:

   Oracle Alert is also considered that has integration with Oracle Payables.

Illustration:

Overview of Payables Integration

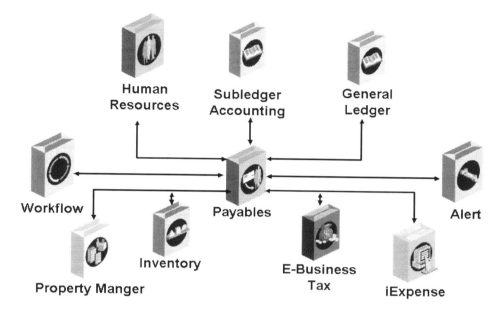

14. It is a predefined workflow that you can initiate to notify managers of transactions incurred by their direct reports. This Workflow determines if workflow will notify a manager of transactions created by the manager's employee's credit card, and it determines if the manager must approve the transactions. What do you call this workflow used in Oracle Payables?

   a.   Credit Card Transaction Manager Workflow
   b.   Expense Report workflow
   c.   Open Interface Import workflow
   d.   Procurement Card Employee Verification workflow

Answer: a

Explanation:

Credit Card workflow - The Credit Card Transaction Manager Workflow is a predefined workflow that you can initiate to notify managers of transactions incurred by their direct reports. The Credit Card Transaction Manager Workflow determines if workflow will notify a manager of transactions created by the manager's employee's credit card, and it determines if the manager must approve the transactions.

Expense Report workflow - The Manager (Spending) Approval Process in the Expense reporting workflow uses the signing limits you define to determine which manager has authority to approve expense reports.

Open Interface Import workflow - Add custom procedures to this workflow to validate invoices entered in the Quick Invoices window. Run the process that starts the workflow prior to running the Payables Open Interface Import program.

Procurement Card Employee Verification workflow - If activated, this workflow sends notifications to employees related to their procurement card transactions. Depending on how the procurement cards are set up, the employee may be required to verify expenditures.

15. **Which of the following is true for Procurement Card Employee Verification Workflow?**

    a. It is a predefined workflow that you can initiate to notify managers of transactions incurred by their direct reports.
    b. If activated, this workflow sends notifications to employees related to their procurement card transactions.
    c. This workflow determines if workflow will notify a manager of transaction created by the manager's employee's credit card, and it determines if the manager must approve the transactions.
    d. This workflow uses the signing limits you define to determine which manager has authority to approve the transactions.

    Answer: b

    Explanation:

    Procurement Card Employee Verification workflow - If activated, this workflow sends notifications to employees related to their procurement card transactions.

    Credit Card workflow - The Credit Card Transaction Manager Workflow is a predefined workflow that you can initiate to notify managers of transactions incurred by their direct reports. The Credit Card Transaction Manager Workflow determines if workflow will notify a manager of transactions created by the manager's employee's credit card, and it determines if the manager must approve the transactions.

    Expense Report workflow - The Manager (Spending) Approval Process in the Expense reporting workflow uses the signing limits you define to determine which manager has authority to approve expense reports.

16. **It is used as an interface to load invoices from a variety of sources including invoices generated from the Pay on Receipt Autoinvoice process, EDI invoices generated by the e-Commerce Gateway, invoices from credit card and procurement card transactions and invoices from external systems. What do you call this payable interface?**

    a. Payables PCard Open Interface
    b. Payables Expense Report Open Interface
    c. Payables Invoice Open Interface
    d. Payables Supplier Open Interface

    Answer: c

    Explanation:

    Payables Invoice Open Interface - Use this interface to load invoices from a variety of sources including invoices generated from the Pay on Receipt Autoinvoice process, EDI invoices generated by the e-Commerce Gateway, invoices from credit card and procurement card transactions and invoices from external systems.

    Payables PCard Open Interface – You can streamline your procure-to-pay process by implementing a procurement card program. Employees purchase items directly from suppliers using a credit card and then the credit card issuer sends transaction files directly to your company. You can import credit card transaction files from your card issuer directly into Payables helping you reduce transaction costs and eliminate low dollar value invoices.

    Payables Expense Report Open Interface - Accounts Payable teams can key paper invoices using the expense reports form or employees can submit their own expense reports using iExpenses. Run the Payables Invoice Import process to validate expense report data and create expense reports in Payables.

    Payables Supplier Open Interface - Use to load supplier data from external systems. You can load suppliers, supplier sites, and supplier contacts using the Payables Supplier Open Interfaces. Once supplier data is loaded, use the Payables Supplier Open Interface Import process to validate them and load them into Payables.

17. **It is used to load supplier data from external systems. You can load suppliers, supplier sites, and supplier contacts using the Payables Supplier Open Interfaces. Once supplier data is loaded, use the Payables Supplier Open Interface Import process to validate them and load them into Payables. What do you call this payable interface?**

   a. Payables PCard Open Interface
   b. Payables Expense Report Open Interface
   c. Payables Invoice Open Interface
   d. Payables Supplier Open Interface

   Answer: d

   Explanation:

   Payables Supplier Open Interface - Use to load supplier data from external systems. You can load suppliers, supplier sites, and supplier contacts using the Payables Supplier Open Interfaces. Once supplier data is loaded, use the Payables Supplier Open Interface Import process to validate them and load them into Payables.

   Payables PCard Open Interface – You can streamline your procure-to-pay process by implementing a procurement card program. Employees purchase items directly from suppliers using a credit card and then the credit card issuer sends transaction files directly to your company. You can import credit card transaction files from your card issuer directly into Payables helping you reduce transaction costs and eliminate low dollar value invoices.

   Payables Expense Report Open Interface - Accounts Payable teams can key paper invoices using the expense reports form or employees can submit their own expense reports using iExpenses. Run the Payables Invoice Import process to validate expense report data and create expense reports in Payables.

   Payables Invoice Open Interface - Use this interface to load invoices from a variety of sources including invoices generated from the Pay on Receipt Autoinvoice process, EDI invoices generated by the e-Commerce Gateway, invoices from credit card and procurement card transactions and invoices from external systems.

18. **In finding supplier, use the search region of the Supplier page to enter a wide variety of search criteria. Which of the following is not part of the search criteria in finding Supplier?**

   a. Supplier Name
   b. Supplier Number
   c. Parent Supplier Name and Number
   d. Tax Registration

   Answer: c

   Explanation:

   In finding Suppliers, use the Search region of the Suppliers page to enter a wide variety of search criteria including:

   1) Supplier Name
   2) Supplier Number
   3) Supplier Type
   4) Tax Registration
   5) DUNS number

   Parent Supplier Name and Number are used to record the relationship between a franchise or subsidiary and its parent company by recording a value for the Parent Supplier Name field. Use the Vendor affiliated Structure Listing to report relationships you've defined.

Illustration:

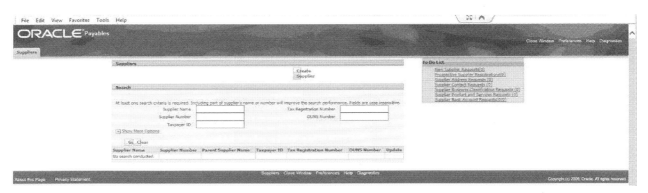

19. **Which of the following is not part of Suppliers: Organization page setup?**

    a. Tax Registration
    b. Customer Number
    c. Parent Supplier Name and Number
    d. Additional Information

    Answer: a

    Explanation:

    Under Suppliers: Organization page setup, you can enter the following information:

    1) Parent Supplier Name and Number
    2) Customer Number
    3) Additional Information

    Tax Registration is entered under Suppliers: Tax Details page.

20. **Which of the following is not part of Suppliers: Tax Details page setup?**

    a. Rounding Rule
    b. Set Invoice Value as Tax Inclusive
    c. Allow Withholding Tax
    d. Parent Supplier Name and Number

    Answer: d

    Explanation:

    Use the Suppliers: Tax Details page to enter tax details and specify withholding applicability. Entry fields are the following:

    1) Rounding Rule
    2) Set Invoice Value as Tax Inclusive
    3) Allow Withholding Tax
    4) Withholding Tax Group
    5) Tax Registration

    Illustration:

Supplier – Tax Details

* Rounding Rule
* Set Invoice Values as Tax Inclusive
* Allow Withholding Tax
* Withholding Tax Group
* Tax Registrations

21. **Which of the following is true for Supplier Audit Report?**

a. Review supplier, supplier site, and supplier site contact information
b. Review supplier payment history, including voided payments, for a supplier or a group of suppliers.
c. Review supplier names that are similar, to help identify potential duplicate suppliers.
d. Review the supplier invoice history, including discount and partial payment information, for a supplier or a group of suppliers.

Answer: c

Explanation:

Supplier Audit Report - Review supplier names that are similar, to help identify potential duplicate suppliers.

Suppliers Report - Review supplier, supplier site, and supplier site contact information.

Supplier Payment History - Review supplier payment history, including voided payments, for a supplier or a group of suppliers.

Supplier Paid Invoice History - Review the supplier invoice history, including discount and partial payment information, for a supplier or a group of suppliers.

22. **It is the default page that the system displays when you initially access the profile details for a Supplier. This page provides access to the main Hold flags for the supplier, along with site-level key purchasing and payment setup attributes. What do you call this page under Supplier setup??**

a. Supplier page
b. Supplier: Quick Update page
c. Suppliers: Organization Page
d. Supplier: Tax and Reporting Page

Answer: b

Explanation:

The Suppliers page provides a central area where you can search for suppliers and provide quick updates to key supplier information. You can also view a TO DO list, which provides a list of pending supplier requests which the suppliers have submitted through Oracle iSupplier Portal.

The Supplier: Quick Update page is the default page that the system displays when you initially access the profile details for a supplier. The page provides access to the main Hold flags for the supplier, along with site-level key purchasing and payment setup attributes.

Use the Suppliers: Organization page to enter Parent Supplier Name and Number, Customer Number and Additional Information.

Use the Supplier: Tax and Reporting page to define the tax profile for your supplier and supplier site.

23. **Enable this option to enable use of the Invoice Batches window, which you can use to specify batch defaults that help speed and control invoice entry in the Invoice Workbench. What profile option is this?**

    a.   AP: Notification Recipient E-mail
    b.   AP: Use Invoice Batch Controls
    c.   AP: Show Finally Closed POs
    d.   PA: Allow Override of PA Distributions in AP/PO

    Answer: b

    Explanation:

    AP: Use Invoice Batch Controls - Enable this option to enable use of the Invoice Batches window, which you can use to specify batch defaults that help speed and control invoice entry in the Invoice Workbench.

    AP: Notification Recipient E-mail - Specify the full e-mail address of the person who will receive notifications from the Concurrent Request Notification program when all the requests in the request set are submitted.

    AP: Show Finally Closed POs - **Yes:** When you are matching, you can view the purchase order numbers of finally closed purchase orders in fields and lists of values in the following windows: Invoice Workbench, Match to Purchase Orders windows, Match to Receipts windows, and the Recurring Invoices window. **No:** Finally closed purchase orders are not displayed during matching and are invalid entries in the windows listed above.

    PA: Allow Override of PA Distributions in AP/PO - This profile option controls whether a user can update the account that the Account Generator generates for project-related distributions.

24. **It is an Oracle Payable profile options where value set to YES, you can view the purchase order numbers of finally closed purchase orders in fields and lists of values in the following windows: Invoice Workbench, Match to Purchase Orders windows, Match to Receipts windows. What profile option is this?**

    a.   AP: Notification Recipient E-mail
    b.   AP: Use Invoice Batch Controls
    c.   AP: Show Finally Closed POs
    d.   PA: Allow Override of PA Distributions in AP/PO

    Answer: c

    Explanation:

    AP: Show Finally Closed POs - **Yes:** When you are matching, you can view the purchase order numbers of finally closed purchase orders in fields and lists of values in the following windows: Invoice Workbench, Match to Purchase Orders windows, Match to Receipts windows, and the Recurring Invoices window. **No:** Finally closed purchase orders are not displayed during matching and are invalid entries in the windows listed above.

    AP: Use Invoice Batch Controls - Enable this option to enable use of the Invoice Batches window, which you can use to specify batch defaults that help speed and control invoice entry in the Invoice Workbench.

AP: Notification Recipient E-mail - Specify the full e-mail address of the person who will receive notifications from the Concurrent Request Notification program when all the requests in the request set are submitted.

PA: Allow Override of PA Distributions in AP/PO - This profile option controls whether a user can update the account that the Account Generator generates for project-related distributions.

25. **It is a Supplier's Tax profile option where when you enable this, you can automatically calculate taxes for a supplier or supplier site. What option is this to set up in Supplier's tax profile?**

   a. Income Tax Reporting Site
   b. Allow Offset Taxes
   c. Set for Self Assessment/Reverse Charge
   d. Allow Tax Applicability

Answer: d

Explanation:

Allow Tax Applicability - Enable this option, if you want to automatically calculate taxes for this supplier or supplier site.

Set for Self Assessment/Reverse Charge - Enable this option if you want to self assess taxes for the supplier or supplier site.

Allow Offset Taxes - Enable this option if you want to allow calculation of offset taxes with this supplier or supplier site.

Income Tax Reporting Site- Enable this option to set the supplier site as the reporting site for a supplier.

26. **In Oracle Payables, which of the following is the correct navigation to setup Payment Terms?**

   a. Setup>Invoice>Payment Terms
   b. Invoices>Payment Terms
   c. Setup>Payment Terms
   d. Setup>Payment>Payment Terms

Answer: a

Explanation:

Correct navigation in setting up Payment Terms is Setup>Invoice>Payment Terms

Illustration:

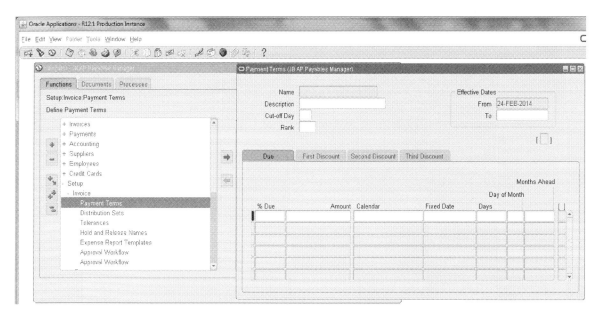

27. In Oracle Payables, which of the following is the correct navigation to setup Supplier?

a. Setup>Supplier
b. Setup>Supplier>Entry
c. Supplier>Entry
d. Setup>Payment>Supplier

Answer: c

Explanation:

Correct navigation in setting up Supplier is Supplier>Entry.

Illustration:

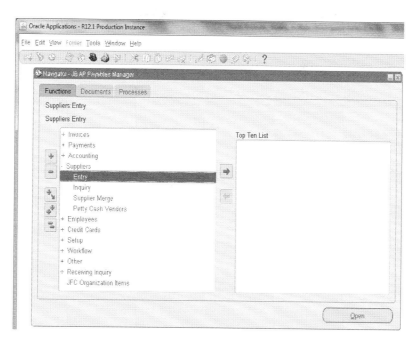

28. **In Oracle Payables, which of the following is the correct navigation to setup Employees?**

a. Setup>Employees
b. Setup>Employees>Entry
c. Employees>Entry
d. Employees>Enter Employees

Answer: d

Explanation:

Correct navigation in setting up Employees is Employees>Enter Employees.

Illustration:

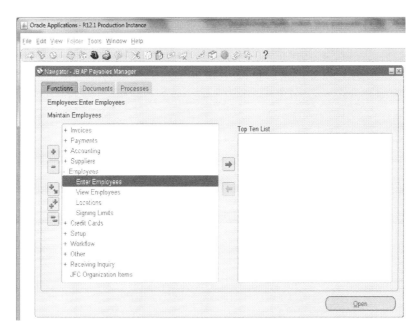

29. **In Oracle Payables, which of the following is the correct navigation to setup Payment Interest Rates?**

    a. Setup>Payment>Interest Rates
    b. Setup>Interest>Rates
    c. Payment>Interest>Rates
    d. Payments>Interest Rates

Answer: a

Explanation:

Correct navigation in setting up Payment Interest Rates is Setup>Payment>Interest Rates.

Illustration:

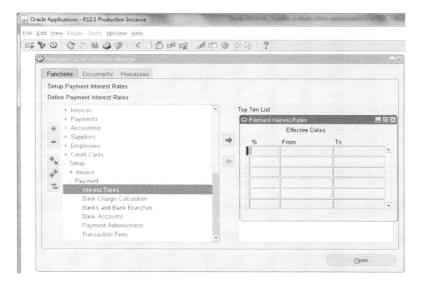

30. **In Oracle Payables, which of the following is the correct navigation to setup Invoice Tolerances?**

a. Setup>Invoice>Tolerances
b. Setup>Invoice Tolerances
c. Payment>Invoice>Tolerances
d. Invoice>Tolerances

Answer: a

Explanation:

Correct navigation in setting up Invoice Tolerances is Setup>Invoice>Tolerances.

Illustration:

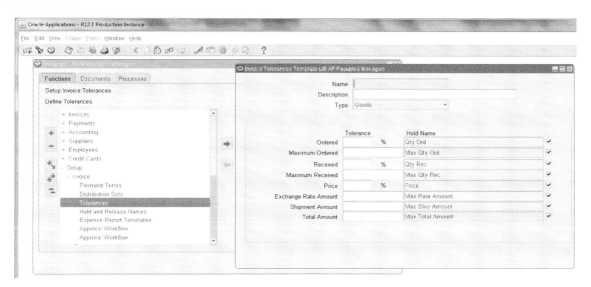

31. **In Key Purchasing Setups of Supplier creation, this field allows you to indicate a preferred carrier that you'd like the supplier to use when shipping to you. What do you call this field?**

a. Ship-to Location/Bill-to Location
b. Ship Via
c. Pay On receipt
d. Alternate Pay Site

Answer: b

Explanation:

Ship Via - allows you to indicate a preferred carrier that you'd like the supplier to use when shipping to you.

Ship-To Location/Bill-To Location - Suppliers generally send invoices and shipments for goods and services to Ship-To and Bill-To Locations. These locations are often not the same.

Pay On Receipt - The Pay on Receipt functionality allows you to create invoices based on receipts and purchase order information in the system. This functionality is generally used with suppliers who send ASNs (Advance Shipment Notices) and ASBNs (Advance Shipping and Billing Notices).

Alternate Pay Site - Pay site to be used as the supplier site when the system creates self-billing invoices for this supplier. This list of values is limited to active pay sites for the supplier.

Invoice Summary Level - The level at which you want to consolidate invoices for this supplier site when you submit the Pay on Receipt AutoInvoice Program.

32. The following are examples of different ways of recording invoices, except for?

a. Import or enter invoices manually, either individually or in batch
b. Use iExpenses to enter employee expense reports using a web browser.
c. Record credit card/procurement card invoices from transactions the credit card issuer sends to you in a flat file.
d. Import PDF Invoices

Answer: d

Explanation:

Using Oracle Payables you can record invoices in different ways, which are:

1) Import or enter invoices manually, either individually or in batches.
2) Use Quick Invoices for rapid, high-volume entry of standard invoices and credit memos that are not complex and do not require extensive online validation.
3) Automate invoice creation for periodic invoices using the Recurring Invoice functionality.
4) Use iExpenses to enter employee expense reports using a web browser.
5) Record credit card/procurement card invoices from transactions the credit card issuer sends to you in a flat file.
6) Import EDI invoices processed with the e-Commerce Gateway.
7) Import lease invoices transferred from Property Manager.
8) Import XML invoices.
9) Match invoices to purchase orders or receipts to ensure you only pay what you're supposed to be paying for.

33. Which of the following is not part of the options of Match Approval Level in Supplier Receiving?

a. 1-Way
b. 2-Way
c. 3-Way
d. 4-Way

Answer: a

Explanation:

Match Approval Level

The Match Approval Level indicates what information will be compared to determine whether an invoice can be validated or not. Options are:

• 2-Way: Purchase order and invoice quantities must match within tolerance before the corresponding invoice can be paid. The receipt close tolerance should be set to 0% to allow the system to automatically close fully received lines.

• 3-Way: Purchase order, receipt, and invoice quantities must match within tolerance before the corresponding invoice can be paid.

- 4-Way: Purchase order, receipt, accepted, and invoice quantities must match within tolerance before the corresponding invoice can be paid.

34. **In Supplier: Invoice Management page, what do you call this field where if you enter an invoice for a supplier site that exceeds a pre-specified invoice amount limit, Payables will automatically place the invoice on an Amount Hold during the Invoice Validation Process?**

    a. Invoice Match Option
    b. Hold All Payments
    c. Invoice Amount Limit
    d. Hold Unvalidated Invoices

    Answer: c

    Explanation:

    Invoice Amount Limit - If you enter an invoice for a supplier site that exceeds a pre-specified invoice amount limit, Payables will automatically place the invoice on an Amount Hold during the Invoice Validation process.

    Invoice Match Option - The Invoice Match Option determines whether or not you intend to match invoices for this supplier against purchase orders or receipts.

    Hold All Payments - Select the Hold All Payments option to prevent any invoices entered for the supplier site from being selected for payment processing.

    Hold Unvalidated Invoices If the Hold Unvalidated Invoices option is selected, Payables will automatically apply a Supplier hold to all invoices as they are entered.

35. **In Invoice Payment Terms, which of the following is not part of the Terms Data Basis list of value (LOV) options?**

    a. Goods Received
    b. Invoice (Date)
    c. Scheduled Ship Date
    d. System (Date)

    Answer: c

    Explanation:

    The following are Terms Date Basis options:

    1) Goods Received
    2) Invoice (Date)
    3) Invoice Received
    4) System (Date)

    Illustration:

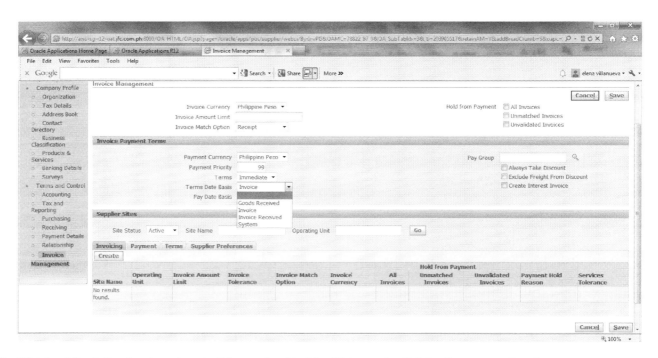

36. **Which of the following is not part of the method in identifying potential duplicate suppliers?**

    a. Submit Supply Payment History Report
    b. Submit and review the Supplier Audit Report
    c. Submit and review the Suppliers Report
    d. Perform a Find or query on the supplier name

    Answer: a

    Explanation:

    Potential duplicate suppliers can be identified through the following methods:

    1) Perform a Find or query on the supplier name
    2) Submit and review the Suppliers Report
    3) Submit and review the Supplier Audit Report to obtain a listing of suppliers whose names are the same up to a specified number of characters
    4) Submit the 1099 Suppliers Exception Report to obtain a listing of suppliers with the same taxpayer ID

37. **What Payable report should be used to review the supplier invoice history, including discount and partial payment information, for a supplier or a group of suppliers?**

    a. Supplier Paid Invoice History
    b. Supplier Audit Report
    c. Supplier Merge Report
    d. Purchase Order Header Updates Report

    Answer: a

    Explanation:

    Supplier Paid Invoice History - Review the supplier invoice history, including discount and partial payment information, for a supplier or a group of suppliers.

Supplier Audit Report - Review supplier names that are similar, to help identify potential duplicate suppliers.

Purchase Order Header Updates Report - Review purchase orders updated by the Supplier Merge Process.

Supplier Merge Report - Review the suppliers, sites, and invoices updated by the Supplier Merge Process.

38. **Which of the following is the correct navigation in setting up Payments System Setup?**

   a. Setup>Options>Payments System Setup
   b. Setup>Payments System Setup
   c. Setup>Payments>Payments System Setup
   d. Payments>Payments System Setup

Answer: a

Explanation:

The correct navigation to setup Payment System Setup is Setup>Options>Payments System Setup.

Illustration:

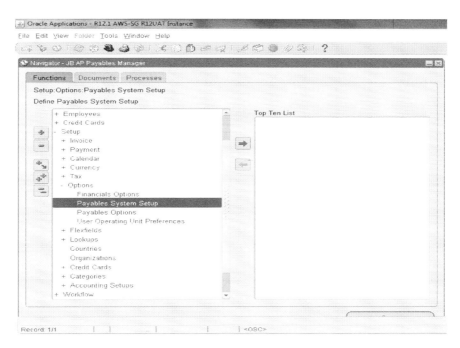

39. **In the Control Payables Periods window, what period status that Payables allows invoice entry and accounting in the future period?**

   a. Open
   b. Closed
   c. Future
   d. Permanently Closed

Answer: c

Explanation:

In the Control Payables Periods window updates the Period Status to one of the following:

Future - Payables allows invoice entry and accounting in a Future period. Payable does not allow payment entry or payment voiding in a Future period.

Payables allows you to limit the number of Future periods based on the number you enter in the Future Periods field in the Financials Options window. After you change the status of a Future period to Open, you cannot change it back to Future.

Open - You can record transactions and account for them in an Open period. You cannot open a period if it is an adjusting period. You define adjusting periods using the Define Calendar window. Adjusting periods can have overlapping dates.

Closed - Payables does not allow transaction processing in a Closed period. You can reopen a Closed period if the corresponding general ledger and purchasing periods are also Open.

Permanently Closed - Payables does not allow transaction processing in a Permanently Closed period. You cannot reopen a Permanently Closed period.

40. **Which of the following is not part the conditions of not being able to close a period in Payables?**

    a. Outstanding Payment Batches
    b. Unaccounted Transaction
    c. Future dated payments for which the Maturity Date is within the period but that still have a status of Issued.
    d. Accounted transactions that have been transferred to general ledger.

    Answer: d

    Explanation:

    You cannot close a period in Payables if any of the following conditions exist:

    Outstanding payment batches. Confirm or cancel all incomplete payment batches.

    Future dated payments for which the Maturity Date is within the period but that still have a status of Issued. Submit the Update Matured Future Payment Status Program.

    Unaccounted transactions. Submit the Create Accounting program to account for transactions, or submit the Unaccounted Transaction Sweep to move any remaining unaccounted transactions from one period to another. See: Creating Accounting Entries in Payables Unaccounted Transactions Sweep.

    Accounted transactions that have not been transferred to general ledger. Transfer accounting entries to General Ledger.

41. **When you enable this option it will mean that you are allowing users to update the distributions of a paid invoice. What do you call this option in Invoice Payable Options?**

    a. Allow Document Category Override
    b. Allow Adjustments to Paid Invoice
    c. Allow Online Validation
    d. Allow Remit-to Account Override

    Answer: b

    Explanation:

Allow Adjustments to Paid Invoices - Enable this option if you want to allow users to update the distributions of a paid invoice. If you enable this option you can also reverse a match to a purchase order document and then match to another purchase order document that is not final matched.

Allow Document Category Override - Enable this option if you want to allow users to override the default Document Category assigned to an invoice by Payables.

Allow Online Validation - Enable this option if you want to allow users to select Invoice Validation from the Invoice Actions window or choose the Validate button in the Invoice Batches window.

Allow Remit-to Account Override - Check this check box if you want to allow users to change the default primary supplier site bank account during Quick payment and payment batch creation. If you enable this option, you can override the Payables default of the Remit-to field of the Payments window and the Modify Payment Batch window.

42. **It is an Invoice Type where an invoice from a supplier representing an amount due for goods or services purchased. What Invoice Type is this?**

    a. Mixed
    b. Standard
    c. Prepayment
    d. Debit Memo

    Answer: b

    Explanation:

    Standard - An invoice from a supplier representing an amount due for goods or services purchased. Standard invoices can be either matched to a purchase order or not matched.

    Debit Memo - An invoice you enter to record a credit for a supplier who does not send you a credit memo.

    Mixed - An invoice type you enter for matching to both purchase orders and invoices. You can enter either a positive or a negative amount for a Mixed invoice type.

    Prepayment - A type of invoice you enter to pay an advance payment for expenses to a supplier or employee.

    Expense Report - An invoice representing an amount due to an employee for business-related expenses.

43. **It is an invoice type you enter for matching to both purchase orders and invoices. You can enter a positive or a negative amount for this invoice type. What do you call this invoice type?**

    a. Prepayment
    b. Expense Report
    c. Mixed
    d. Debit Memo

    Answer: c

    Explanation:

Mixed - An invoice type you enter for matching to both purchase orders and invoices. You can enter either a positive or a negative amount for a Mixed invoice type.

Prepayment - A type of invoice you enter to pay an advance payment for expenses to a supplier or employee.

Expense Report - An invoice representing an amount due to an employee for business-related expenses.

Debit Memo - An invoice you enter to record a credit for a supplier who does not send you a credit memo.

44. **It is an Invoice Type used for recording the difference in price between the original invoice and the new purchase order price. This Invoice type can be matched to both purchase order and invoices. What Invoice Type is this?**

    a. PO Price Adjustment Invoices
    b. Standard
    c. Prepayment
    d. Expense Report

    Answer: a

    Explanation:

    PO Price Adjustment Invoices are for recording the difference in price between the original invoice and the new purchase order price. PO price adjustment invoices can be matched to both purchase orders and invoices.

    Standard - An invoice from a supplier representing an amount due for goods or services purchased. Standard invoices can be either matched to a purchase order or not matched.

    Prepayment - A type of invoice you enter to pay an advance payment for expenses to a supplier or employee.

    Expense Report - An invoice representing an amount due to an employee for business-related expenses.

45. **It is an element of basic invoice structure that defines the common information about the invoice such as invoice number and date, supplier information, remittance information and payment terms. What do you call this element?**

    a. Invoice Header
    b. Invoice Lines
    c. Scheduled Payments
    d. Distribution

    Answer: a

    Explanation:

    Invoice header defines the common information about the invoice: invoice number and date, supplier information, remittance information, and payment terms

    Invoice lines define the details of the goods and services as well as the tax, freight, and miscellaneous charges invoiced by the supplier. There can be multiple invoice lines for each invoice header.

    Scheduled payments are created based on payment terms when the invoice header is saved.

Distribution details include invoice accounting details, the GL date, charge accounts and project information. An invoice line can have one or more invoice distributions.

46. Which of the following is the correct navigation in creating Invoice Batches?

a. Setup>Invoices>Invoice Batches
b. Invoices>Entry>Invoices>Batches
c. Invoices>Entry>Invoice Batches
d. Setup>Invoices>Entry>Invoice Batches

Answer: c

Explanation:

The correct navigation in creating Invoice Batches is Invoices>Entry>Invoice Batches.

Illustration:

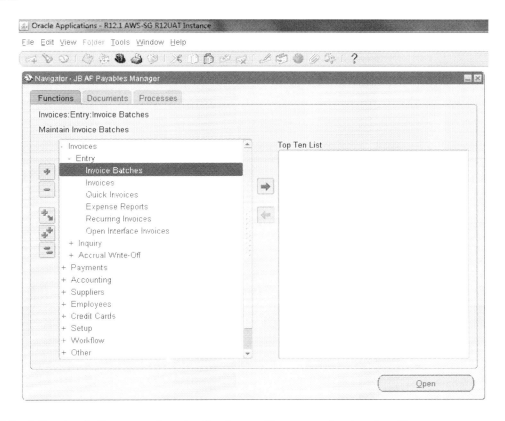

47. Which of the following is the correct navigation in creating Recurring Invoices?

a. Invoices>Entry>Recurring Invoices
b. Invoices>Entry>Invoices>Recurring Invoices
c. Setup>Invoices>Entry>Recurring Invoices
d. Setup>Invoices>>Recurring Invoices

Answer: a

Explanation:

The correct navigation in creating Invoice Batches is Invoices>Entry>Recurring Invoices.

Illustration:

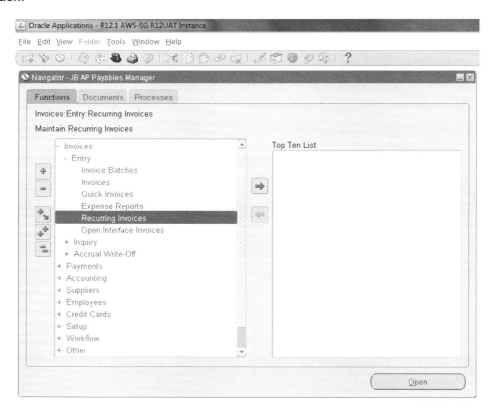

48. **Which of the following is the correct navigation for Invoice Batches Inquiry?**

a. Invoices>Inquiry>Entry>Invoice Batches
b. Invoices>Inquiry>Invoice Batches
c. Setup>Invoices>Inquiry>Invoice Batches
d. Setup>Invoices>>Invoice Batches

Answer: b

Explanation:

The correct navigation to access Invoice Batch inquiry is Invoices>Inquiry>Invoice Batches.

Illustration:

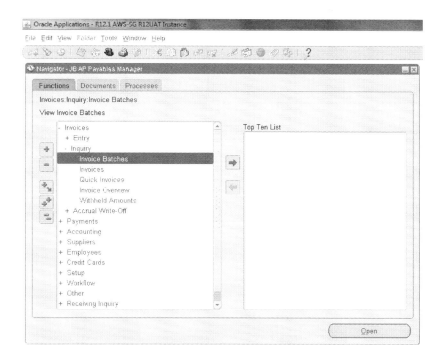

49. **Which of the following types of invoice lines that captures the details of the goods and services billed on your invoice?**

    a. Tax Lines
    b. Freight and Miscellaneous Lines
    c. Item Lines
    d. None of the above

    Answer: c

    Explanation:

    Different types of invoice lines are:
    1) Item Lines - capture the details of the goods and services billed on your invoice.
    2) Freight lines capture the details of your freight charges. Freight charges can be allocated to Item lines as required.
    3) Miscellaneous lines capture the details of other charges on your invoices such as installation or service.
    4) Tax lines - Payables integrates with Oracle E-Business Tax to automatically determine and calculate the applicable tax lines for your invoices.

50. **There are three ways to create freight distributions. Which of the following is not one of the three ways?**

    a. Enable the Automatically Create Freight Distribution Payables Option
    b. Allocate freight across invoice distribution
    c. Manually enter freight distributions
    d. Import Freight Distribution

    Answer: d

    Explanation:

Three ways to create freight distribution:

1) Enable the Automatically Create Freight Distribution Payables Option
2) Allocate freight across invoice distribution
3) Manually enter freight distributions

51. **It is an allocation restriction of Invoices where you cannot adjust an allocation after you have accounted for the charge. What do you call this allocation restriction of invoices?**

    a. Cancelled Invoices
    b. Paid Invoices
    c. Items matched to multiple PO distribution
    d. Accounted allocations

Answer: d

Explanation:

Allocation Restriction

Cancelled Invoices - You cannot modify allocations if the invoice is cancelled.

Paid invoices - If the invoice is partially or fully paid and the Allow Adjustments to Paid Invoices Payables option is not enabled, you cannot create new charges in the Allocations window.

Applied prepayments - If a Prepayment invoice has been partially or fully applied, you cannot create new charges in the Allocations window.

Items matched to multiple PO distributions - Multiple Item distributions, each matched to a different PO distribution, cannot receive allocations from a single non-recoverable Tax distribution.

Accounted allocations - You cannot adjust an allocation after you have accounted for the charge.

52. **In allocation restriction of Invoices, which of the following in not true?**

    a. You cannot modify allocation if the invoice is cancelled.
    b. If the invoice is partially or fully paid and the Allow Adjustments to Paid Invoices Payable option is not enabled, you cannot create new charges in the Allocation window.
    c. If Prepayment invoice has been partially or fully applied, you cannot create new charges in the Allocation window.
    d. You can adjust an allocation after you have accounted for the charge.

Answer: d

Explanation:

Allocation Restriction

Cancelled Invoices - You cannot modify allocations if the invoice is cancelled.

Paid invoices - If the invoice is partially or fully paid and the Allow Adjustments to Paid Invoices Payables option is not enabled, you cannot create new charges in the Allocations window.

Applied prepayments - If a Prepayment invoice has been partially or fully applied, you cannot create new charges in the Allocations window.

Items matched to multiple PO distributions - Multiple Item distributions, each matched to a different PO distribution, cannot receive allocations from a single non-recoverable Tax distribution.

Accounted allocations - You cannot adjust an allocation after you have accounted for the charge.

53. **In Invoice Workbench, which of the following Tab or Region where you can hold the payment to a Supplier?**

a.   General
b.   Lines
c.   Holds
d.   Scheduled Payments

Answer: d

Explanation:

The Schedule Payments Tab of Invoice Workbench is where you can hold payment to a supplier.

Illustration:

General Tab

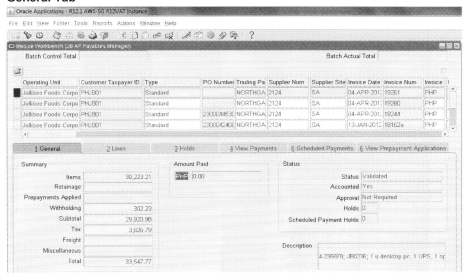

Line Tab

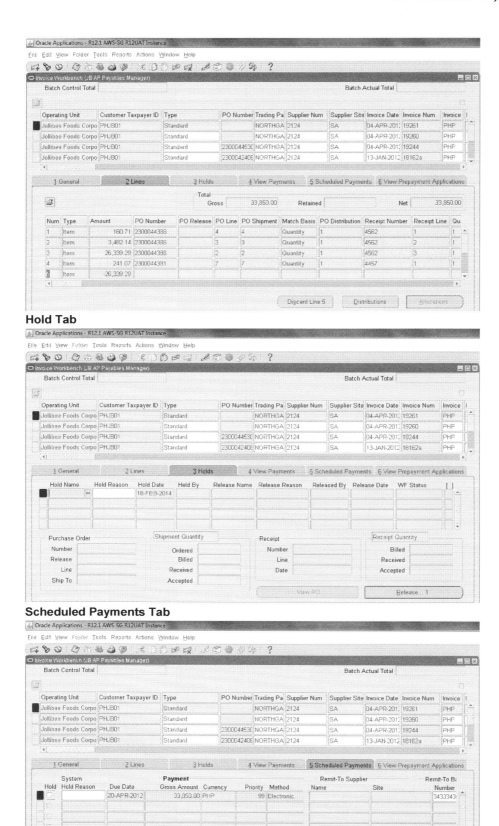

Hold Tab

Scheduled Payments Tab

54. **Which of the following is not true for reason to use match to receipt?**

a. Matching to receipts allows you to pay only for goods you receive.
b. Any exchange rate variance that results from matching is likely to be smaller because the time between the receipt and invoice will probably be less than the time between the purchase order and invoice.
c. Matching to receipts allows you to distribute allocation to Invoices.
d. Matching an invoice for freight or miscellaneous charges to a material receipt is required for accurate costing data if you use periodic costing.

Answer: c

Explanation:

Reasons to use match to receipt:

1) Matching to receipts allows you to pay only for goods you receive.
2) Any exchange rate variance that results from matching is likely to be smaller because the time between the receipt and invoice will probably be less than the time between the purchase order and invoice.
3) Matching an invoice for freight or miscellaneous charges to a material receipt is required for accurate costing data if you use periodic costing.

55. **Which of the following is not true for reason to use price correction?**

a. You use price correction to override the unit price when matching an invoice to a purchase order.
b. You use a price correction when a supplier sends an invoice for a change in unit price for an invoice you have already matched to a purchase order. If you simply enter an invoice for a unit price increase or a credit/debit memo for a unit price decrease without using price correction, invoice price variances will not be accurate.
c. You can enter and match an invoice to record a price increase, or you can enter and match a credit memo or debit memo to record a price decrease.
d. Use a price correction to adjust the invoiced unit price of previously matched purchase order shipments, distributions, or receipts without adjusting the quantity billed.

Answer: a

Explanation:

Reasons to user Price Correction:

1) You use a price correction when a supplier sends an invoice for a change in unit price for an invoice you have already matched to a purchase order. If you simply enter an invoice for a unit price increase or a credit/debit memo for a unit price decrease without using price correction, invoice price variances will not be accurate.
2) You can enter and match an invoice to record a price increase, or you can enter and match a credit memo or debit memo to record a price decrease.
3) Use a price correction to adjust the invoiced unit price of previously matched purchase order shipments, distributions, or receipts without adjusting the quantity billed.

56. **Which of the following is the correct navigation to setup Withholding Tax Code?**

a. Setup>Tax>Withholding>Code
b. Tax>Withholding>Code
c. Setup>Tax>Withholding
d. Setup>Withholding>Tax>Code

Answer: a

Explanation:

The correct navigation to setup Withholding Tax Details is Setup>Tax>Withholding>Code.

Illustration:

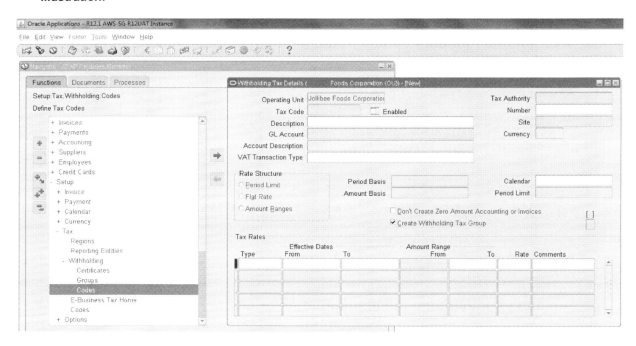

57. **In Payables Options window, when you update or reset the Payment Term to Net 30 from Net 45, which of the following is TRUE for the new 50 Supplier and with existing suppliers?**

   a. The 50 new Suppliers will have Net 30 Payment Term and existing Suppliers will have Payment Term Net 45.
   b. The 50 new Suppliers will have Net 30 Payment Term and existing Suppliers will have Payment Term Net 30.
   c. The 50 new Suppliers will have Net 45 Payment Term and existing Suppliers will have Payment Term Net 45.
   d. The 50 new Suppliers will have Net 45 Payment Term and existing Suppliers will have Payment Term Net 30.

Answer: a

Explanation:

Changes to default values affect only new records, not existing records. For example, if payment terms in the Payables Options window are reset to Net 30 from Net 45, new suppliers will have a default of Net 30. Existing suppliers will have terms of Net 45.

58. **Which of the following is not TRUE for creating invoices automatically?**

   a. Recurring Invoices
   b. Customer Sales Invoices
   c. Return to Supplier (RTS) Invoices
   d. Retroactive Price Adjustment Invoices

Answer: b

Explanation:

Creating Invoices Automatically

1) Recurring Invoices - You can set up your system to automatically create periodic invoices, for example, rent invoices.
2) RTS Invoices - If you use Return to Supplier feature in Oracle Purchasing, the system creates these debit memos directly in your Payables system.
3) Retroactive Price Adjustment Invoices - If Oracle Purchasing users use the Retroactive Pricing of Purchase Orders feature, the system automatically creates Adjustment and PO Price Adjustment invoices.

Customer Sales Invoices is not part of creating invoices automatically. These invoices are only used for Receivables transaction.

59. **In the Invoice Structure, which of the following is true for Invoice Header?**

    a. The invoice header defines the details of the goods and services as well as the tax, freight, and miscellaneous charges invoiced by the supplier.
    b. The invoice header defines the Invoice payment details including scheduled payment date, amount and priority.
    c. The invoice header defines details include invoice accounting details, the GL date, charge accounts, and project information. An invoice line can have one or more invoice distributions.
    d. The invoice header defines the common information about the invoice: invoice number and date, supplier information, remittance information, and payment terms.

    Answer: d

    Explanation:

    In the Invoice Structure, the invoice header defines the common information about the invoice: invoice number and date, supplier information, remittance information, and payment terms. Information specified at the invoice header level defaults down to the line level. You can override the header level information for individual lines, as required.

60. **The primary window in the Invoice Workbench is the Invoices window. The Invoices window is divided into regions. Which of the following items has complete list of Invoices window regions?**

    a. Invoice Header, Lines, Holds, View Payments, Schedule Payments and View Prepayment Applications.
    b. General, Lines, Holds, View Payments, Schedule Payments and View Prepayment Applications.
    c. Invoice Header, General, Lines, Holds, View Payments, Schedule Payments and View Prepayment Applications.
    d. Invoice Header, General, Holds, View Payments, Schedule Payments and View Prepayment Applications.

    Answer: c

    Explanation:

    The primary window in the Invoice Workbench is the Invoices window. The Invoices window is divided into the following regions:

    1) Invoice Header
    2) General
    3) Lines
    4) Holds
    5) View Payments
    6) Scheduled Payments
    7) View Prepayment Applications

61. Which of the following is the correct navigation in creating Expense Reports?

    a.   Setup>Invoices>Entry>Expense Reports.
    b.   Invoices>Entry>Expense Reports
    c.   Setup>Invoices> Expense Reports
    d.   Setup> Expense Reports

Answer: b

Explanation:

The correct navigation in creating Expense Reports is Invoices>Entry>Expense Reports

Illustration:

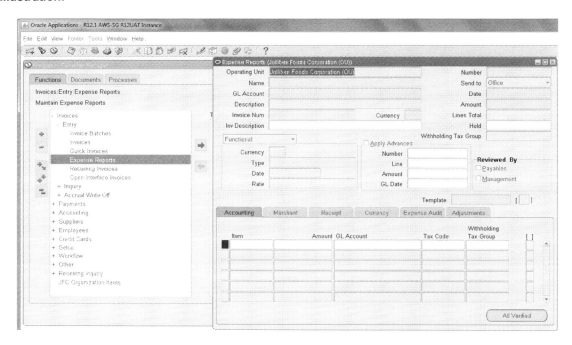

62. Which of the following is the correct navigation in creating Recurring Invoices?

    a.   Setup>Invoices>Entry> Recurring Expenses
    b.   Invoices>Entry>Recurring Expenses
    c.   Setup>Invoices> Recurring Expenses
    d.   Setup> Recurring Expenses

Answer: b

Explanation:

The correct navigation to create Recurring Expenses is Invoices>Entry>Recurring Expenses.

Illustration:

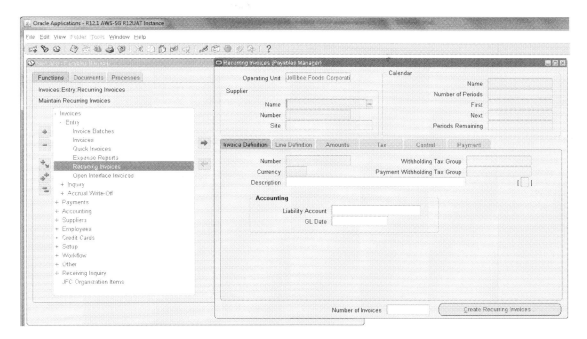

63. **Which of the following is the correct navigation in creating Open Interface Invoices?**

   a. Setup>Invoices>Entry> Open Interface Invoices
   b. Invoices>Entry> Open Interface Invoices
   c. Setup>Invoices> Open Interface Invoices
   d. Setup> Open Interface Invoices

Answer: b

Explanation:

The correct navigation in creating Open Interface Invoices is Invoices>Entry> Open Interface Invoices.

Illustration:

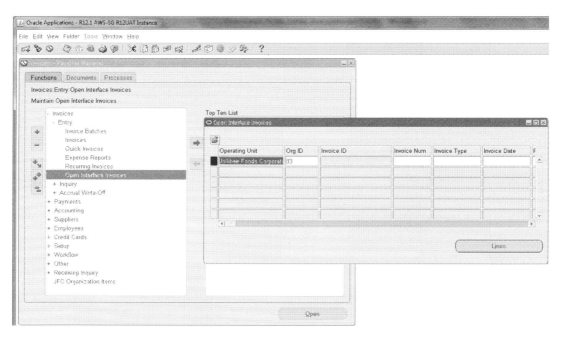

64. **Which of the following is the correct navigation to View Write-offs?**

    a.   Invoices>View Write-Offs
    b.   Setup>Invoices> View Write-Offs
    c.   Invoices>Accrual Write-Off>View Write-Offs
    d.   Setup> View Write-Offs

Answer: c

Explanation:

The correct navigation in executing View Write-Off is Invoices>Accrual>View Write-Offs.

Illustration:

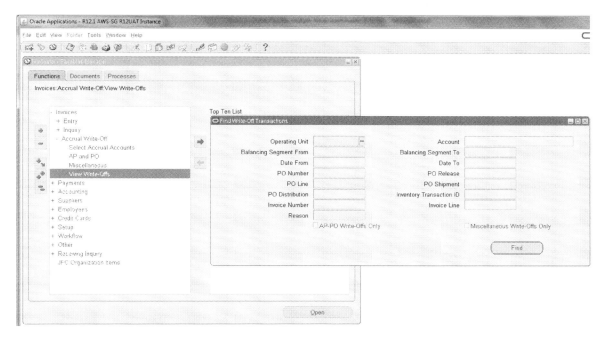

65. **Which of the following is the correct navigation to Select Accrual Accounts?**

a.   Invoices>Select Accrual Accounts
b.   Setup>Invoices> Accrual Write-Off>Select Accrual Accounts
c.   Invoices>Accrual Write-Off>Select Accrual Accounts
d.   Setup>Select Accrual Accounts

Answer: c

Explanation:

The correct navigation in creating Select Accrual Accounts is Invoices>Accrual Write-Off>Select Accrual Accounts.

Illustration:

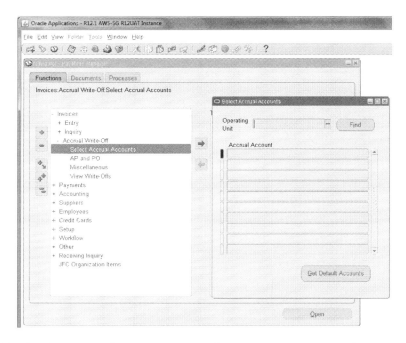

66. **Which of the following is not true for prerequisites of Invoice Approval Workflow Program?**

    a. Define all your invoice approval rules in Oracle Approvals Management (OAM).
    b. Set up, and optionally customize, the Invoice Approval Workflow.
    c. Enable the Use Invoice Approval Workflow Payables option.
    d. An invoice does not meet all selection criteria.

    Answer: d

    Explanation:

    Prerequisites of Invoice Approval Workflow Program

    1) Define all your invoice approval rules in Oracle Approvals Management (OAM).
    2) Set up, and optionally customize, the Invoice Approval Workflow.
    3) Enable the Use Invoice Approval Workflow Payables option.
    4) Each invoice meets all selection criteria.
    5) In the Submit Requests window your system administrator should schedule the Workflow Agent Listener to run regularly.

67. **It is an Oracle Payable report used to view unpaid invoices and provides information about invoice payments due within four time periods. This report does not included cancelled invoices. What report is this?**

    a. Invoice Audit Listing by Voucher Number
    b. Invoice Aging Report
    c. Invoice Audit Listing
    d. Credit Memo Matching Report

    Answer: b

    Explanation:

Invoice Aging Report - Use this report to view your unpaid invoices. This report provides information about invoice payments due within four time periods you specify in the Aging Periods window. This report does not included cancelled invoices.

Invoice Audit Listing by Voucher Number- Use this report to review your invoices with assigned sequential voucher numbers. Either you or Payables can assign a unique, sequential number to an invoice during invoice entry, if you enable the Sequential Numbering profile option.

Invoice Audit Listing - Use the Invoice Audit Listing to audit invoices for duplicates. You should audit invoices periodically to ensure control of invoice payments. You can sort this listing in six different ways. You can also use this report to obtain a listing of your invoices by invoice type.

Credit Memo Matching Report This report lists credit memos and debit memos that match the supplier and date parameters you specify. The report also lists the total of the distribution line amounts of each credit memo in your entered currency and your functional currency.

68. **It is an Oracle Payable report that helps you to quickly identify and review a detailed list of all activities pertaining to a specific invoice including all payments, gain/loss, credit/debit memos and discounts. What report is this?**

   a. Invoice on Hold Report
   b. Invoice Audit Report
   c. Invoice History Report
   d. Invoice Register

   Answer: c

   Explanation:

   Invoice History Report - The Invoice History Report is needed to justify the balance for a given range of invoices. It helps you to quickly identify and review a detailed list of all activities pertaining to a specific invoice including all payments, gain/loss, credit/debit memos, and discounts. The balance of the invoices is then summed for each supplier site, for each supplier, and for the entire report.

   Invoice on Hold Report - Use the Invoice on Hold Report to review detailed information about invoices on hold.

   Invoice Audit Report - Use the Invoice Audit Report to audit invoices for duplicates. The report lists invoices that appear as potential duplicates according to several criteria.

   Invoice Register - Use the Invoice Register to review detailed information about invoices. You can also use this report to view the offsetting liability accounts that Payables creates for each invoice distribution when you validate an invoice. Payables orders the report by invoice currency and, if you use batch control, the invoice batch name then by supplier name and invoice number.

69. **It is an Oracle Payable report used to send to a supplier to inform them about one or more invoices you have entered. You can generate this report from either the Invoices window or the Submit Requests window.**

   a. Recurring Invoices Report
   b. Matching Hold Agent Notice
   c. Print Invoice Notice
   d. Supplier Paid Invoice History

   Answer: c

   Explanation:

Print Invoice Notice - Generate a standard invoice notice to send to a supplier to inform them about one or more invoices you have entered. For credit/debit memos, the notice informs the supplier of outstanding credit or debit memos that you will apply to future invoices. You can generate this report from either the Invoices window or the Submit Requests window. You can use Reports to change the boilerplate text.

Recurring Invoices Report - Use this report to review recurring invoice templates you defined during a specific time period. You can review this report to determine the amount you have authorized for a recurring invoice template, how much you have released, and the next amount you have scheduled.

Matching Hold Agent Notice - Use the Matching Hold Agent Notice to print a notice informing a purchasing agent of any matching holds due to a variance between an invoice and the agent's purchase order. When you submit this report, Payables prints a notice to each purchasing agent who has issued a purchase order that has a variance with its matched invoice.

Supplier Paid Invoice History - You can submit the Supplier Paid Invoice History Report by supplier or supplier type to review payment history, discounts taken, and frequency of partial payments.

70. **Which of the following is the correct navigation to setup Payables System Setup?**

   a.   Setups>Options>Payables System Setup
   b.   Setup>Payables System Setup
   c.   Setups>Invoices>Options>Payables System Setup
   d.   Invoices>Options>Payables System Setup

Answer: a

Explanation:

The correct navigation in setting-up Payables System Setup is Setups>Options>Payables System Setup.

Illustration:

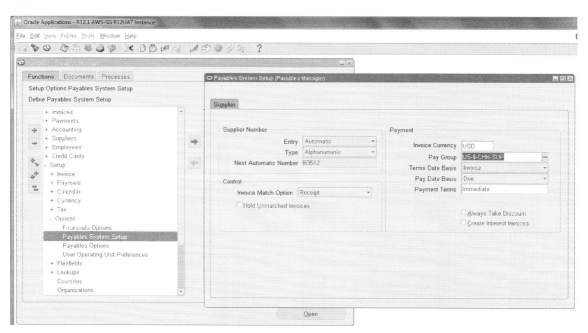

71. Which of the following is the correct navigation to setup Financials Options?

a. Setups>Financials Options
b. Invoices> Financials Options
c. Setups>Invoices>Options> Financials Options
d. Setups>Options>Financials Options

Answer: d

Explanation:

The correct navigation in setting-up Financials Options is Setups>Options>Financials Options.

Illustration:

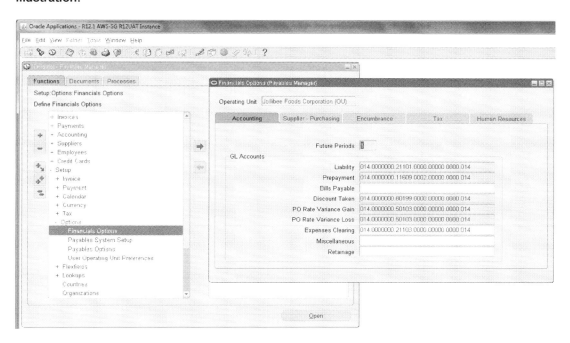

72. Which of the following is the correct navigation to setup Financials Options?

a. Setups>Payables Options
b. Invoices>Payables Options
c. Setups>Invoices>Options> Payables Options
d. Setups>Options>Payables Options

Answer: d

Explanation:

The correct navigation in setting-up Financials Options is Setups>Options>Payables Options.

Illustration:

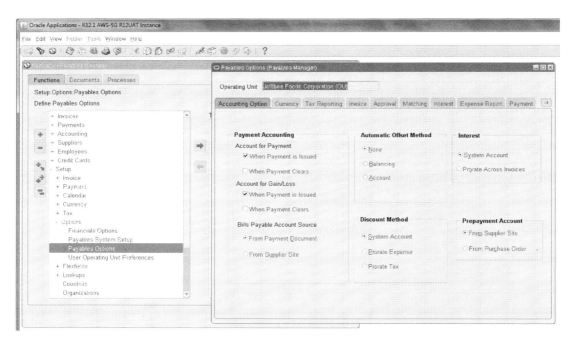

73. **In Accounting Option section of Payable Option, which of the following is the correct and complete Discount Method Options?**

a. System Account, Prorate Across Invoices, Prorate Expense
b. System Account, Prorate Expense, Prorate Tax
c. System Account, Prorate Expense, Prorate Across Invoices
d. System Account, Prorate Across Invoices, Prorate Tax

Answer: b

Explanation:

Discount Method Options are:

1) System Account
2) Prorate Expense
3) Prorate Tax

Illustration:

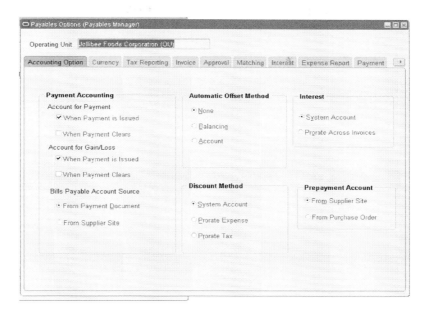

74. **Oracle Payables lists four seeded payment methods. They are check, outsourced check, electronic, and wire. Which of the following statement is true for wire?**

a. A paper check to print and send to a supplier
b. An EFT, EDI, or XML to the bank of a supplier
c. A funds transfer initiated by contacting the bank and requesting wire payment to the bank of a supplier
d. Transmission of payment information to an external party, such as your bank, that prints checks on your behalf

Answer: c

Explanation:

Wire is a funds transfer initiated by contacting the bank and requesting wire payment to the bank of a supplier.

Illustration:

Seeded Payment Methods

Payment Method	Definition
Check	A paper check to print and send to a supplier
Outsourced Check	Transmission of payment information to an external party, such as your bank, that prints checks on your behalf
Electronic	An EFT, EDI, or XML payment to the bank of a supplier
Wire	A funds transfer initiated by contacting the bank and requesting wire payment to the bank of a supplier

75. **Which of the following method is not true for an invoice can be submitted for validation?**

a. Online by clicking the Validate button in the Invoice Batches window
b. Online by clicking the Validate and Account button in the Invoice Batches window
c. In batch by submitting the Payables Invoice Validation program from the Invoice Workbench
d. Online by selecting either the Validate check box or the Validate Related Invoices check box in the Invoice Actions window

Answer: b

Explanation:

Three ways that an invoice can be submitted for validation:

1) Online by clicking the Validate button in the Invoice Batches window
2) In batch by submitting the Payables Invoice Validation program from the Submit Request window
3) Online by selecting either the Validate check box or the Validate Related Invoices check box in the Invoice Actions window

76. **Identify the four setup options that control supplier defaults.**

a. Financial options
b. Receiving options
c. Purchasing options
d. Payables system setup

Answer: c

Explanation:

Use the Payable System Setup Options to define the general supplier defaults for Payables. You can define supplier- and supplier site-specific defaults in the Suppliers page.

Use Financials Options to define Supplier defaults across all Oracle Financials applications, including Payables. You can define supplier- and supplier site-specific defaults in the Suppliers page.

Use the Purchasing options to define the supplier defaults, such as freight terms and shipping details, on requisitions, purchase orders, requests for quotations, etc.

Use the Receiving Options to define options that govern receipts in your system. Receiving Options has nothing to do with Supplier Defaults.

77. **Which of the following setup options that cannot be define in the Financial Option window?**

   a. Interest and expense AP accrual account
   b. Retainage
   c. Miscellaneous
   d. Expenses clearing

Answer: a

Explanation:

Financial Options window setups:

1) Future Periods
2) Liability
3) Prepayment
4) Bills Payable
5) Discount taken
6) PO Rate Variance Gain
7) PO Rate Variance Loss
8) Expense Clearing
9) Miscellaneous
10) Retainage

Illustration:

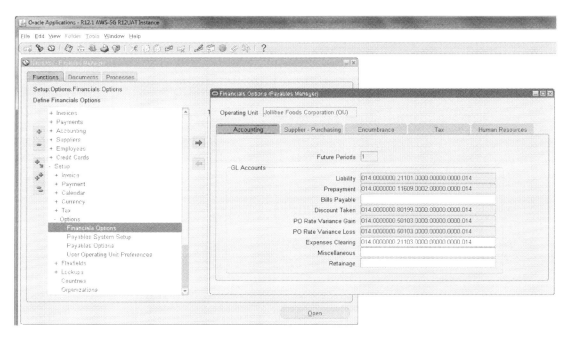

78. **In allocating Freight and Miscellaneous distributions, which of the following you do in Charge Allocation window?**

   a.   Create and allocate freight or miscellaneous charge distributions to item distributions.

   b.   Review and update existing allocations for a charge.

   c.   Partially allocate a charge. The amount must be fully allocated before you can save the allocation.

   d.   Allocate an existing freight or miscellaneous charge distribution to one or more distributions to record costs for Periodic Costing.

Answer: c

Explanation:

Allocating Freight and Miscellaneous Distributions

You can use the Charge Allocations window to:

1) Create and allocate freight or miscellaneous charge distributions to item distributions.
2) Allocate an existing freight or miscellaneous charge distribution to one or more distributions to record costs for Periodic Costing.
3) Review and update existing allocations for a charge.

You cannot:

1) Allocate any distribution to itself.
2) Allocate an item distribution to any other distribution type.
3) Allocate freight or miscellaneous charges to tax lines.
4) Partially allocate a charge. The amount must be fully allocated before you can save the allocation.

79. **Which of the following statement is not true for matching to distribution for Assets?**

    a. The charge account on the purchase order for an item that will be capitalized and depreciated is a balance sheet account and will be a clearing account associated with an asset category (like COMPUTER-PC) in Assets.
    b. After matching, the asset clearing account will be on the distribution for the invoice.
    c. When the asset is prepared and posted to Assets, the clearing account is cleared and the asset cost account associated with the asset category is charged for the cost of the asset.
    d. Payables will transfer the AP accrual account to the general ledger and Assets will transfer the clearing account clearing entry and the asset cost entry.

    Answer: d

    Explanation:

    The charge account on the purchase order for an item that will be capitalized and depreciated is a balance sheet account and will be a clearing account associated with an asset category (like COMPUTER-PC) in Assets. After matching, the asset clearing account will be on the distribution for the invoice. When the asset is prepared and posted to Assets, the clearing account is cleared and the asset cost account associated with the asset category is charged for the cost of the asset. Payables will transfer the asset clearing account to the general ledger and Assets will transfer the clearing account clearing entry and the asset cost entry.

80. **In Matching, tab/section of Payable Options, which of the following statement is true for Allow Distribution Level Matching?**

    a. Select this option if you want to allow matching to purchase order distributions.
    b. Select this option, if you can match an invoice to one or more purchase order distributions.
    c. Do not select this option, if you can match an invoice to a purchase order Shipment.
    d. Select this option, if you can match an invoice to a purchase order Shipment.

    Answer: d

    Explanation:

    Allow Distribution Level Matching. Select this option if you want to allow matching to purchase order distributions. If you select this option, you can match an invoice to one or more purchase order distributions. If you do not select this option, you can match an invoice to a purchase order Shipment.

81. **Which of the following is not true for Matching to Distributions for Expenses?**

    a. The charge account on the purchase order for an item that will be expensed (for example, office supplies) is an income statement account.
    b. After matching, the expense account is transferred to the invoice distribution if you are accruing at period end.
    c. When accounting is transferred to the general ledger, the amount charged to the expense account can be reported on the balance statement.
    d. When accounting is transferred to the general ledger, the amount charged to the expense account can be reported on the income statement.

Answer: c

Explanation:

Matching to Distributions for Expenses

The charge account on the purchase order for an item that will be expensed (for example, office supplies) is an income statement account. After matching, the expense account is transferred to the invoice distribution if you are accruing at period end. When accounting is transferred to the general ledger, the amount charged to the expense account can be reported on the income statement.

82. **What does it mean if the FINAL_MATCH_FLAG of table AP_INVOICE_DISTRIBUTION_ALL becomes "Y" after you match an invoice to a purchase order?**

    a. The PO shipment line has not been matched.
    b. The PO shipment line has been matched, and one of the invoices for this PO has been final matched. When a PO is final matched to an invoice, all other invoices matched to that PO are updated, too. So, you cannot tell from this flag, which invoice was final matched.
    c. The PO shipment line is closed. You cannot invoice this distribution line.
    d. The PO shipment line is purged.

    Answer: b

    Explanation:

    FINAL_MATCH_FLAG of table AP_INVOICE_DISTRIBUTION_ALL has the following quick codes values which are:

    N - No. The PO shipment line has not been matched.

    Y - Yes. The PO shipment line has been matched, and one of the invoices for this PO has been final matched. When a PO is final matched to an invoice, all other invoices matched to that PO are updated, too. So, you cannot tell from this flag, which invoice was final matched.

    D - Done. The PO shipment line is closed. You cannot invoice this distribution line.

83. **Purchase order matched invoices are invoices that you match to any of the following, except for.**

    a. Purchase order shipments and receipts
    b. Purchase order with status Request for approval.
    c. Purchase order receipt lines
    d. Purchase order distributions

    Answer: b

    Explanation:

    Purchase order matched invoices are invoices that you match to any of the following:

1) Purchase order shipments
2) Purchase Order receipts
3) Purchase order receipt lines
4) Purchase order distributions

84. **Which of the following statement is not true for Matching to Distributions for Inventory?**

a. The charge account on the purchase order for an item that will be capitalized as inventory is a balance sheet account and will be a material clearing account associated with an inventory organization in Inventory.
b. After matching, the Inventory AP Accrual Account will be on the distribution for the invoice.
c. When the receipt is processed the AP Accrual Account (uninvoiced receipts account) is credited.
d. When booking the invoice and matching, the receipt is now invoiced and the balance in the Asset Clearing Account must be cleared.

Answer: c

Explanation:

Matching to Distributions for Inventory

The charge account on the purchase order for an item that will be capitalized as inventory is a balance sheet account and will be a material clearing account associated with an inventory organization in Inventory. After matching, the Inventory AP Accrual Account will be on the distribution for the invoice. When the receipt is processed the AP Accrual Account (uninvoiced receipts account) is credited. When booking the invoice and matching, the receipt is now invoiced and the balance in the AP Accrual Account must be cleared. At receipt, Purchasing will transfer the accrual to the AP Accrual Account (a credit) and after matching, Payables will transfer the clearing entry to the AP Accrual Account as part of the Transfer Journals to GL process.

85. **Payable creates the following accounting entries after payment reconciliation or clearing in Cash Management but except for?**

a. Reconciled payment: debit the Cash Clearing account and credit the Cash account
b. Unreconciled payment: debit the AP Liability account and credit the Cash Clearing account
c. Bank charges: debit the Bank Charges account and credit the Cash account
d. Bank errors: account in Cash account and Bank Errors account. Debits and credits depend whether the bank error was a positive or negative amount

Answer: b

Explanation:

Payables then create the following accounting entries after payment reconciliation or clearing in Cash Management:

1) Reconciled payment: debit the Cash Clearing account and credit the Cash account
2) Bank charges: debit the Bank Charges account and credit the Cash account
3) Bank errors: account in Cash account and Bank Errors account. Debits and credits depend whether the bank error was a positive or negative amount

Payables creates the following accounting entries after payment issue:

Unreconciled payment: debit the AP Liability account and credit the Cash Clearing account.

86. **If you select When Payments Clears option solely, payables create accounting entries after you clear the payment in Oracle Cash Management. Which of the following accounting entries is NOT true for When Payments Clears option?**

    a. Reconciled payment: debit the AP Liability account and credit the Cash (asset) account.
    b. Bank charges: debit the Bank Charges account and credit the Cash account.
    c. Unreconciled payment: debit the AP Liability account and credit the Cash account.
    d. Bank errors: account in Cash account and Bank Errors account. Debits and credits depend whether the bank error was a positive or negative amount.

    Answer: c

    Explanation:

    When Payment Clears. If you select only this option, Payables accounts for each payment once, after clearing. After you clear the payment in Oracle Cash Management, Payables creates the following accounting entries.

    1) Reconciled payment: debit the AP Liability account and credit the Cash (asset) account.
    2) Bank charges: debit the Bank Charges account and credit the Cash account.
    3) Bank errors: account in Cash account and Bank Errors account. Debits and credits depend whether the bank error was a positive or negative amount.

    When Payment is Issued: Payables accounts for each payment once, after payment issue. After you issue the payment, Payables creates the following accounting entries.

    1) Unreconciled payment: debit the AP Liability account and credit the Cash account.

87. **Which of the following is the correct navigation in setting-up Employee Signing Limits?**

    a. Setup>Employee>Signing Limits
    b. Supplier>Employee>Signing Limits
    c. Employee>Singing>Limits>Amount
    d. Employee>Signing Limits

    Answer: d

    Explanation:

    The correct navigation in going to Employee Signing Limits setup is Employee>Signing Limits.

    Illustration:

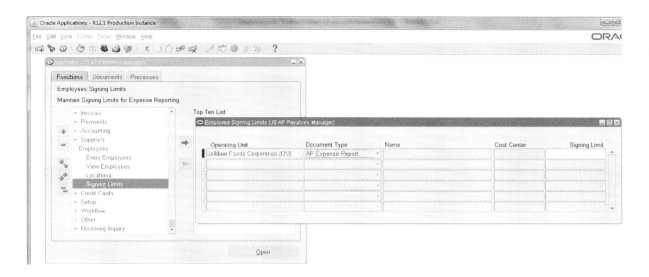

88. Which of the following is the correct navigation for setting-up Card Programs?

a. Setup>Credit Cards>Card Programs
b. Credit Cards>Card Programs
c. Setup>Payments>Credit Cards>Card Programs
d. Supplier>Credit Cards>Card Programs

Answer: a

Explanation:

The correct navigation to setup Card Programs is Setup>Credit Cards>Card Programs.

Illustration:

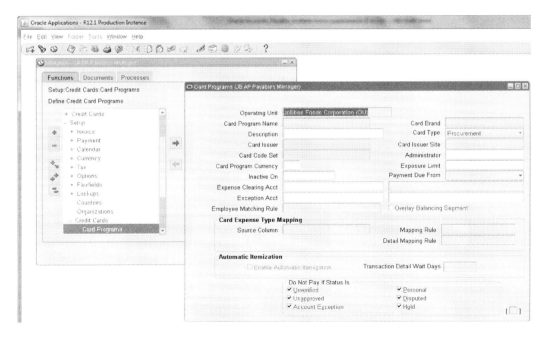

89. **Which of the following is the correct navigation for setting-up Expense Report Template?**

    a. Setup>Expense>Expense Report Template
    b. Invoice>Expense Report Template
    c. Setup>Invoice>Expense Report Templates
    d. Payment>Expense Report Template

Answer: c

Explanation:

The correct navigation to Expense Report Template setup is Setup>Invoice>Expense Report Templates.

Illustration:

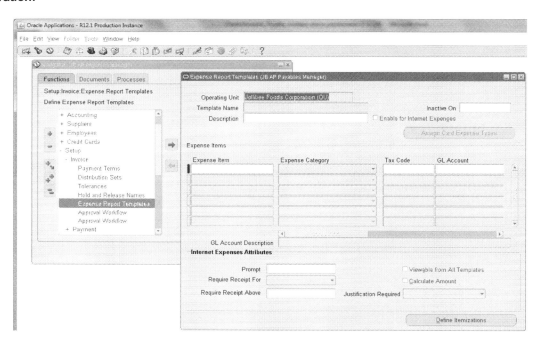

90. **Which of the following is the correct navigation for setting-up Transaction Fees?**

    a. Setup>Banks>Transaction Fees
    b. Invoice>Banks>Transaction Fees
    c. Setup>Invoice>Transaction Fees
    d. Setup>Payment>Transaction Fees

Answer: d

Explanation:

The correct navigation to Transaction Fees setup is Setup>Payment>Transaction Fees.

Illustration:

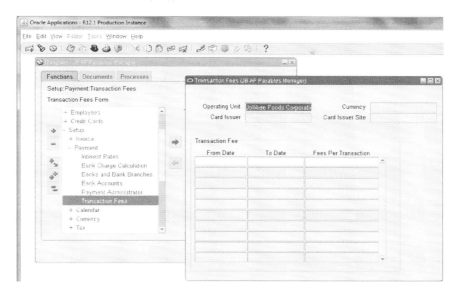

91. **Which of the following is the correct navigation for setting-up Subledger Application?**

a. Setup>Accounting Setup>Subledger Accounting Setup>Subledger Application

b. Setup>Accounting Setup>Ledger Setup>Subledger Application

c. Setup> Subledger Accounting Setup>Subledger Application

d. Setup> Ledger Setup>Subledger Application

Answer: a

Explanation:

The correct navigation in setting up Subledger Application is Setup>Accounting Setup>Subledger Accounting Setup>Subledger Application.

Illustration:

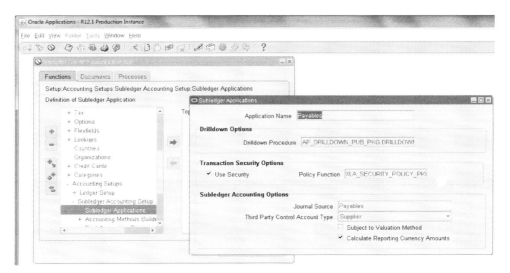

92. **Which of the following statement is not true for Calculate Reporting Currency Amounts?**

    a. If selected, the Create Accounting program calculates accounted amounts and creates journals for all enabled subledger level reporting currencies associated with the primary ledgers.
    b. If not selected, the Create Accounting program does not calculate accounted amount for any reporting currencies, but it does create journals for the subledger level reporting currencies if reporting currency information is provided in the transaction objects.
    c. If the Create Accounting program fails to create journal entries for any of the subledger level reporting currencies, no journal entries are created for the primary and secondary ledgers and for other subledger level reporting currencies.
    d. Calculate Reporting Currency Amounts option can be apply to secondary ledgers.

    Answer: d

    Explanation:

    Calculate Reporting Currency Amounts option:

    1) If selected, the Create Accounting program calculates accounted amounts and creates journals for all enabled subledger level reporting currencies associated with the primary ledgers.
    2) If not selected, the Create Accounting program does not calculate accounted amount for any reporting currencies, but it does create journals for the subledger level reporting currencies if reporting currency information is provided in the transaction objects.
    3) If the Create Accounting program fails to create journal entries for any of the subledger level reporting currencies, no journal entries are created for the primary and secondary ledgers and for other subledger level reporting currencies.
    4) This option does not apply to secondary ledgers. The Financial Services Accounting Hub calculates accounted amount for secondary ledgers regardless of the value of the Calculate Reporting Currency Amounts option.

93. **Which of the following statement is not true for Payment Process Profiles?**

    a. Payment process profile is a blueprint assigned to document payable.
    b. The purpose of payment process profile is to specify the details of the payment process.
    c. Funds disbursement payment methods, Formats and Payment systems and transmission configurations are the prerequisite setups for Payment Process Profiles.
    d. Payment process profile is a setup that controls the accounting entries for Payments.

    Answer: d

    Explanation:

    Payment Process Profile define as a blueprint assigned to document payable, which specify

    1) All the rules for creating and disbursing payments
    2) How payments are process
    3) Instruction for payment formatting and transmission.

    The purpose of payment process profile is to specify the details of the payment process.

Illustration:

Setting Up Payment Process Profiles

A payment process profile is a blueprint assigned to documents payable, which specifies:

* all the rules for creating and disbursing payments
* how payments are processed
* instructions for payment formatting and transmission

The purpose of setting up payment process profiles is to specify the details of the payment process.

94. Which of the following statement is not true for Payment Systems?

a. Payment systems is used to define the external organization that process your funds disbursement transactions

b. Payment systems is used defines the deploying company's relationships with its payment systems.

c. Payment systems requirements setup is transmission configurations only.

d. Payment system is an organization that provides financial services.

Answer: c

Explanation:

The purpose of setting up payment systems is to define:

1) The external organizations that process your funds disbursement transactions
2) The deploying company's relationships with its payment systems

Prerequisites before you can set up payment systems, you must setup the following:

1) Formats
2) Transmission configurations

Illustration:

Setting Up Payment Systems

A payment system is an organization that provides financial settlement services, such as a:

- bank at which the deploying company has its bank accounts
- third party processor that connects deploying companies with financial institutions

95. **Which of the following is the correct navigation to setup Approval Workflow for invoice?**

a. Invoice>Approval Workflow

b. Setup>Invoice>Approval Workflow

c. Payment>Invoice>Approval Workflow

d. Workflow>Invoice>Approval Workflow

Answer: b

Explanation:

The correct navigation to setup Approval Workflow is Setup>Invoice>Approval Workflow.

Illustration:

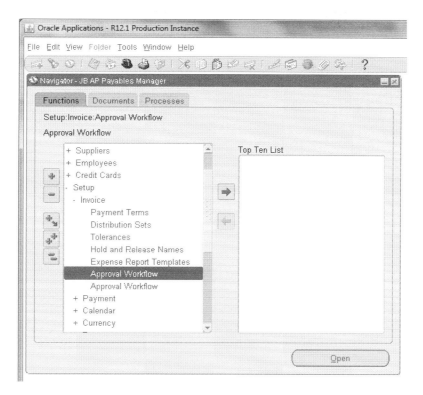

96. Which of the following is the correct navigation to setup Calendar Periods in Oracle Payable?

a. Setup>Calendar>Periods
b. Setup>Accounting>Periods
c. Setup>Calendar>Accounting>Periods
d. Setup>Payable Options>Calendar>Periods

Answer: c

Explanation:

The correct navigation to setup Calendar Periods is Setup>Calendar>Accounting>Periods.

Illustration:

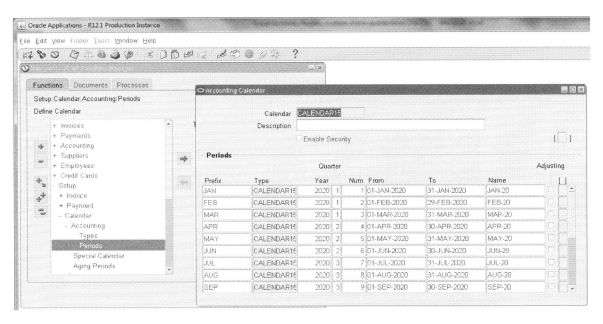

97. Which of the following is the correct navigation to setup Special Calendar in Oracle Payable?

a. Setup>Calendar>Special Calendar
b. Setup>Accounting>Special Calendar
c. Setup>Calendar>Accounting>Special Calendar
d. Setup>Payable Options>Calendar>Special Calendar

Answer: a

Explanation:

The correct navigation to setup Special Calendar in Oracle Payable is Setup>Calendar>Periods.

Illustration:

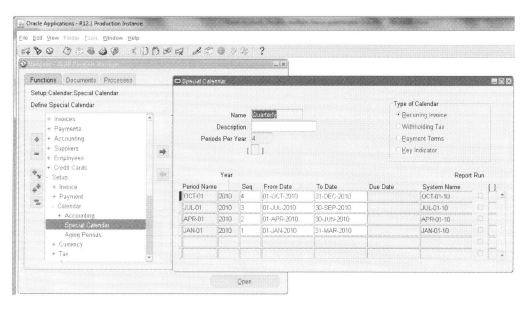

98. **Which of the following is the correct navigation to setup Aging Periods in Oracle Payable?**

   a. Setup>Calendar>Aging Periods
   b. Setup>Accounting>Aging Periods
   c. Setup>Calendar>Accounting>Aging Periods
   d. Setup>Payable Options>Calendar>Aging Periods

Answer: a

Explanation:

The correct navigation to setup Aging Periods in Oracle Payable is Setup>Calendar>Aging Periods.

Illustration:

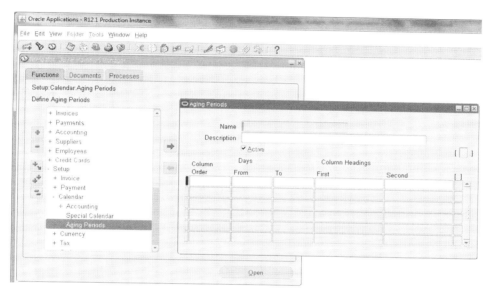

99. **Which of the following is the correct navigation to setup Category Codes in Oracle Payable?**

   a. Setup>Categories>Category Codes
   b. Setup>Categories>Codes>Category Codes
   c. Setup>Categories>Accounting>Category Codes
   d. Setup>Payable Options>Categories>Category Codes

Answer: a

Explanation:

The correct navigation to setup Category Codes in Oracle Payable is Setup>Categories>Category Codes.

Illustration:

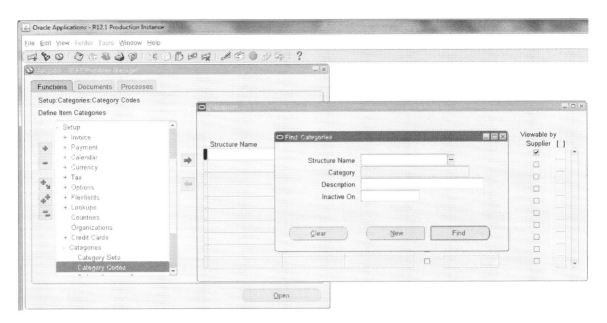

100.In the Special Calendar window, which of the following is not type of calendar?

a. Recurring Invoice
b. Discount Terms
c. Withholding Tax
d. Payment Terms

Answer: b

Explanation:

In the Special Calendar window, the following are options for selecting Type of Calendar:

1) Recurring Invoice
2) Withholding Tax
3) Payment Terms
4) Key Indicator

Illustration:

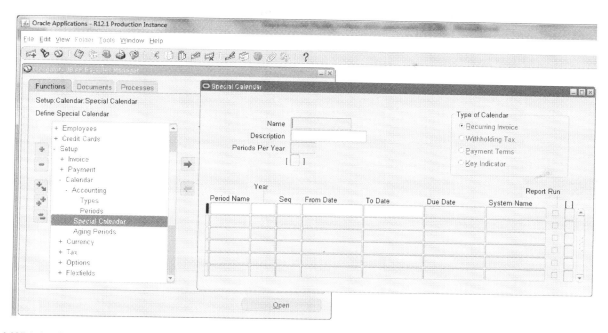

101. Which of the following is not part of Payables Period Closing process?

a. Prepare for period close
b. Open next period
c. Create Accounting
d. Close the GL Period

Answer: b

Explanation:

Payables Period Closing process:

1) Prepare for period close
2) Run validation/review and resolve holds
3) Create accounting
4) Transfer and review unaccounted transactions
5) Close the period
6) Post Journal entries in GL
7) Reconcile AP activity for the period
8) Close the GL Period

Illustration:

Overview of the Period Close

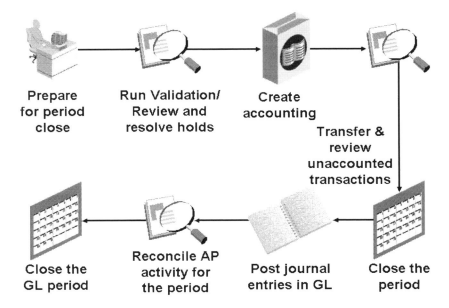

102. In Transaction Distribution Window of Procurement Card Transactions, which of the following is not a status of the transaction?

    a.   Approved
    b.   Disputed
    c.   Verified
    d.   Entered

Answer: b

Explanation:

Complete transaction status in Transaction Distribution window:

1) Approved
2) Disputed
3) Hold
4) Personal
5) Rejected
6) Validated
7) Verified

103. Which of the following is the correct navigation in setting up Procurement Card Transactions?

    a.   Setup>Procurement Card Transactions
    b.   Setup>Invoice>Procurement Card Transactions
    c.   Credit Cards>Procurement Card Transactions
    d.   Setup>Credit Cards>Procurement Card Transactions

Answer: c

Explanation:

The correct navigation in setting up a Procurement Card Transactions is Credit Cards>Procurement Card Transactions

Illustration:

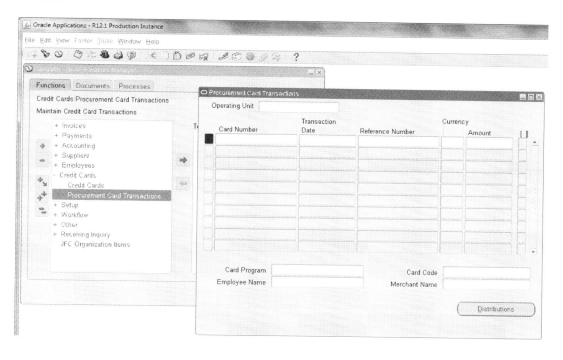

104.**Which of the following is not true for Preparing for Period Close?**

a.   Complete all receipts processing
b.   Import Invoices
c.   Update matured bills payable
d.   Confirm or cancel closed pay runs

Answer: d

Explanation:

The following are complete list for Preparing for Period Close:

1)   Complete all receipts processing
2)   Confirm or cancel all pending pay runs
3)   Update matured bills payable
4)   Import Invoices

5) Export and process expense reports
6) Reconcile Bank Statement

105. Which of the following statement is not true for advantages of Oracle Internet Expenses?

a. It reconciles payments from Payables and updates status of reconciled payments.
b. It reduces administrative costs and data entry errors since data entry is streamlined and accessible anywhere online (mobile, desktop, browser) or offline (spreadsheet).
c. It eliminates expensive IT customizations through global accommodation for local statutory regulations and automates audit management, conserving staff for analytical work and providing better information to management.
d. It increases productivity when employees can flexibly create expense reports using a standard Web browser, a connected Web-enabled mobile device, a disconnected spreadsheet, and or downloaded credit card transactions.

Answer: a

Explanation:

Advantages of Oracle Internet Expenses

1) It reduces administrative costs and data entry errors since data entry is streamlined and accessible anywhere online (mobile, desktop, browser) or offline (spreadsheet).
2) It enforces spend policy to control expenses, showing any policy deviations.
3) It eliminates expensive IT customizations through global accommodation for local statutory regulations and automates audit management, conserving staff for analytical work and providing better information to management.
4) It increases productivity when employees can flexibly create expense reports using a standard Web browser, a connected Web-enabled mobile device, a disconnected spreadsheet, and or downloaded credit card transactions.
5) It improves cycle times by routing expense reports via workflow to managers for approval and to accounts payable department for reimbursement.
6) It increases employee satisfaction when their status-related questions can be selfanswered within the application.

Reconciles payments from Payables and updates status of reconciled payments is a definition of Oracle Cash Management.

106. In Payment Window, you can adjust selected invoices for manual payments and:

a. Adjust a manual payment used to pay a prepayment that was applied to an invoice
b. Make any changes to cleared o or voided payments
c. Make adjustments to selected invoices on matured bills payable if accounting exists for the maturity event
d. Update manual payment addresses

Answer: d

Explanation:

You can use the Payment Window to:

1) Adjust selected invoices for Manual payments
2) Update Manual payments addresses

You cannot perform the following update payment actions:

1) Adjust a manual payment used to pay a prepayment that was applied to an invoice
2) Make any changes to cleared o or voided payments
3) Make adjustments to selected invoices on matured bills payable if accounting exists for the maturity event

107. **Which of the following is not a recording print status of prenumbered payment documents?**

a. Setup
b. Printed
c. Skipped
d. Error

Answer: d

Explanation:

Recording print status of prenumbered payment documents:

1) Setup
2) Printed
3) Skipped
4) Spoiled
5) Overflow

108. **It is recording print status of prenumbered payment documents where the printer malfunctioned (jammed or missed a check) and ruined these documents, so you cannot reuse them. What do you call this print status of prenumbered payment documents?**

a. Setup
b. Printed
c. Skipped
d. Spoiled

Answer: d

Explanation:

1) Setup: Payments automatically displays the setup checks used to align your printer.
2) Printed: The documents printed properly.
3) Skipped: The printer skipped over these documents and nothing printed on them. You can reuse these documents for single payments.

4) Spoiled: The printer malfunctioned (jammed or missed a check) and ruined these documents, so you cannot reuse them. Documents may also be spoiled if the wrong payment document was used. Payments automatically void these documents when you record them as spoiled.

5) Overflow: You may have check overflow, a situation where there are more invoices paid by a check than can fit on the remittance advice of one check. All the documents are displayed on the payment table, and should be marked accordingly.

109. You can review the following in the Scheduled Payment Selection Report, except for?

a. Invoices selected for a pay run

b. Debit missed

c. Invoice selection criteria

d. Immediate cash requirements for the pay run

Answer: b

Explanation:

You can review the following in the Scheduled Payment Selection Report:

1) Invoices selected for a pay run

2) Invoice selection criteria

3) Immediate cash requirements for the pay run

4) Credit missed

5) Available prepayments

6) Unselected invoices

110. What reports are available to check if a credit memo is matched to an invoice?

a. Matching Detail Report

b. Credit Memo Matching Report

c. Expense Report

d. Immediate cash requirements for the pay run

Answer: b

Explanation:

In Payables, run the Credit Memo Matching Report from Other > Request > Run. Credit Memo Matching Report is a report in Oracle Payables used to check if a credit memo is matched to an invoice.

Matching Detail Report is an Oracle Payable report that will show you detail of how an invoice, purchase order, or receipt was matched. This report is especially helpful when an invoice is on hold and you are trying determining why the hold was placed.

Expense Report is an invoice representing an amount due to an employee for business-related expenses.

Invalid PO Supplier Notice Report is an Oracle Payable report used to inform a supplier that you placed an invoice on hold because the supplier did not provide a purchase order number for matching, or you could not use the purchase order number provided by the supplier

111. **How can I find out which invoices are matched to a Purchase Order?**

    a. Matching Detail Report

    b. Credit Memo Matching Report

    c. Expense Report

    d. Immediate cash requirements for the pay run

Answer: b

Explanation:

In Payables, run the Matching Detail Report from Other > Request > Run. Matching Detail Report is an Oracle Payable report that will show you detail of how an invoice, purchase order, or receipt was matched. This report is especially helpful when an invoice is on hold and you are trying determining why the hold was placed.

Credit Memo Matching Report is a report in Oracle Payables used to check if a credit memo is matched to an invoice.

Expense Report is an invoice representing an amount due to an employee for business-related expenses.

Invalid PO Supplier Notice Report is an Oracle Payable report used to inform a supplier that you placed an invoice on hold because the supplier did not provide a purchase order number for matching, or you could not use the purchase order number provided by the supplier.

112. **In Payables, the important setup steps are Matching Options and Tolerances. Which option you select to allow final matching of purchase order matched invoices? Using this option, you can indicate a final match when you match an invoice to a purchase order during invoice entry or when you adjust a matched invoice distribution.**

    a. Allow Final Matching

    b. Allow Distribution Level Matching

    c. Allow Matching Account Override

    d. Transfer PO Descriptive Flexfield Information.

Answer: a

Explanation:

Matching Options and Tolerances

Allow Final Matching - Select this option to allow final matching of purchase order matched invoices. You can indicate a final match when you match an invoice to a purchase order during invoice entry or when you adjust a matched invoice distribution. Select this option only if you want to allow the option of permanently closing the purchase orders. Once a purchase order is permanently closed, you cannot reopen the purchase orders.

Allow Distribution Level Matching - Select this option if you want to allow matching to purchase order distributions. If you select this option, you can match an invoice to one or more purchase order distributions. If you do not select this option, you can match an invoice to a purchase order Shipment.

Allow Matching Account Override - Select this option if you want to allow override of the account for an invoice distribution created from matching to a purchase order. You can override the account for a matched invoice distribution in the Distributions window.

Transfer PO Descriptive Flexfield Information - Select this option if you want to automatically transfer the descriptive flexfield information from the purchase order distribution to the invoice distributions when you match an invoice to a purchase order.

Illustration:

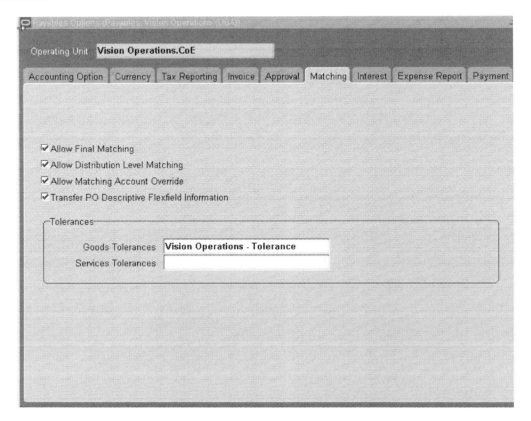

113. **Which of the following statement is not true for Allow Distribution Level Matching?**

    a.   Select this option to allow final matching of purchase order matched invoices.
    b.   Select this option if you want to allow matching to purchase order distributions.
    c.   If you select this option, you can match an invoice to one or more purchase order distributions.
    d.   If you do not select this option, you can match an invoice to a purchase order Shipment.

Answer: a

Explanation:

Allow Distribution Level Matching - Select this option if you want to allow matching to purchase order distributions. If you select this option, you can match an invoice to one or more purchase order distributions. If you do not select this option, you can match an invoice to a purchase order Shipment.

114. **Which of the following navigation to direct you to setup or enable/disable option Exclude Tax from Discount Calculation?**

    a.   Setup>Options>Payable Options>Payments
    b.   Setup>Options>Financial Options>Payments
    c.   Setup>Payment>Payments
    d.   Setup>Invoice>Payments

Answer: a

Explanation:

The correct navigation to direct you to setup or enable/disable the option Exclude Tax from Discount Calculation is Setup>Options>Payable Options>Payments.

Illustration:

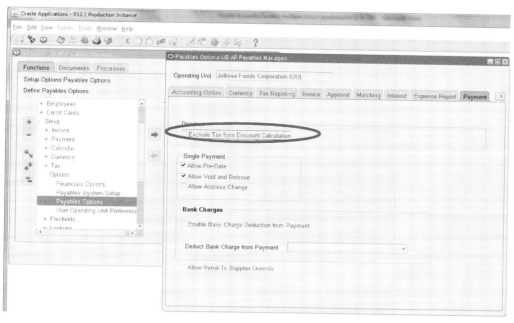

115. If you enable this option then you can report on federal income tax withheld (MISC4) for 1099 suppliers. Which of the following navigation to direct you to enable or disable "Include Income Tax Type on Withholding Distributions" option?

   a. Setup>Options>Payment Options>Withholding Tax>Include Income Tax Type as Withholding Distributions
   b. Setup>Options>Financial Options>Withholding Tax>Include Income Tax Type as Withholding Distributions
   c. Setup>Tax>Withholding Tax>Include Income Tax Type as Withholding Distributions
   d. Setup>Withholding Tax>Include Income Tax Type as Withholding Distributions

Answer: a

Explanation:

The correct navigation to enable and disable the option Include Income Tax Type on Withholding Distributions is Setup>Options>Payment Options>Withholding Tax>Include Income Tax Type as Withholding Distributions.

Illustration:

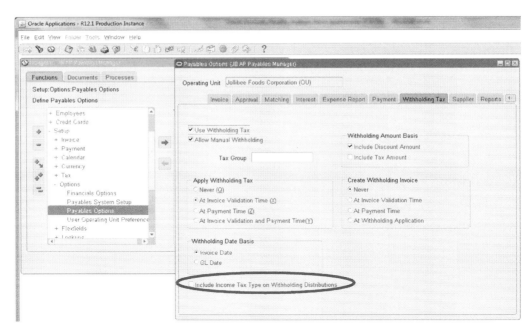

116. **Which of the following Invoice Payable Options that if you enable this, then during invoice entry when you accept the invoice date as the default for invoice number, Payable displays a pop-up window that reads "Use the Invoice Date as the Invoice Number?**

    a. Allow Online Validation
    b. Allow Document Category Override
    c. Allow Adjustments to Paid Invoices
    d. Confirm Date as Invoice Number

Answer: d

Explanation:

Confirm Date as Invoice Number. If you enable this option, then during invoice entry when you accept the invoice date as the default for invoice number, Payables displays a pop-up window that reads, "Use the Invoice Date as the Invoice Number?"

Allow Online Validation. Enable this option if you want to allow users to select Invoice Validation from the Invoice Actions window or choose the Validate button in the Invoice Batches window.

Allow Document Category Override. Enable this option if you want to allow users to override the default Document Category assigned to an invoice by Payables.

Allow Adjustments to Paid Invoices. Enable this option if you want to allow users to update the distributions of a paid invoice.

Illustration:

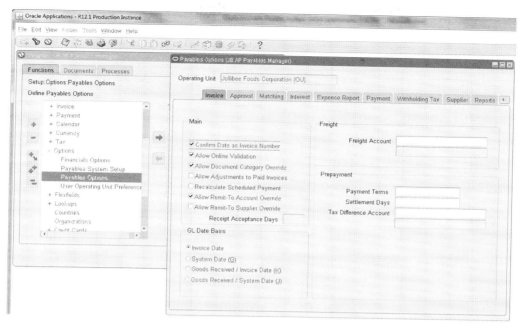

117. **Which of the following Invoice Payable Options that if you enable this option you want to allow users to update the distribution of a paid invoice?**

    a. Allow Online Validation
    b. Allow Document Category Override
    c. Allow Adjustments to Paid Invoices
    d. Confirm Date as Invoice Number

    Answer: c

    Explanation:

    Allow Adjustments to Paid Invoices. Enable this option if you want to allow users to update the distributions of a paid invoice.

    Allow Online Validation. Enable this option if you want to allow users to select Invoice Validation from the Invoice Actions window or choose the Validate button in the Invoice Batches window.

    Confirm Date as Invoice Number. If you enable this option, then during invoice entry when you accept the invoice date as the default for invoice number, Payables displays a pop-up window that reads, "Use the Invoice Date as the Invoice Number?"

    Allow Document Category Override. Enable this option if you want to allow users to override the default Document Category assigned to an invoice by Payables.

118. **The Oracle Payables application (AP) includes the Payments Workbench - an entry form (stored on the Forms Server) which allows users to record "Manual" payments (made outside of Oracle), create single "Quick" payments to creditors, record single "Refund" payments received from creditors, view existing payments and?**

    a. generate the Cash Requirements Report
    b. manage existing payments (including entering stops and voids)
    c. manually submit single payment batches

d.   create pre-defined templates to speed up manual payment batch entry and facilitate automatic scheduling of payment batches

Answer: b

Explanation:

The Oracle Payables application (AP) includes the Payments Workbench - an entry form (stored on the Forms Server) which allows users to:

1)   record "Manual" payments (made outside of Oracle)
2)   create single "Quick" payments to creditors
3)   record single "Refund" payments received from creditors
4)   view existing payments
5)   manage existing payments (including entering stops and voids)

The Oracle Payments application (IBY) includes the Payments Manager-- an entry form (stored on the Web Server) which allows users to:

1)   generate the Cash Requirements Report
2)   manually submit single payment batches
3)   create pre-defined templates to speed up manual payment batch entry and facilitate automatic scheduling of payment batches

119. For example, you are closing your accounting period for April and you have just posted your final invoice and payment batches to your general ledger system. To reconcile your accounts payable activity for April, which of the following calculation will you use?

a.   April Accounts Payable Trial Balance = April Accounts Payable Trial Balance
                                  + April Posted Invoice Register
                                  - April Posted Payment Register

b.   April Accounts Payable Trial Balance = March Accounts Payable Trial Balance
                                  + April Posted Invoice Register
                                  - April Posted Payment Register

c.   April Accounts Payable Trial Balance = March Accounts Payable Trial Balance
                                  + April Unposted Invoice Register
                                  - April Posted Payment Register

d.   April Accounts Payable Trial Balance = March Accounts Payable Trial Balance
                                  + April Unposted Invoice Register
                                  - April Unosted Payment Register

Answer: b

Explanation:

Reconciling Accounts Payable Trial Balance for a given period

Add the current period's posted invoices (total invoice amount from the Posted Invoice Register) and subtract the current period's posted payments (total cash plus discounts taken from the Posted Payments Register) from the prior period's Accounts Payable Trial Balance. This amount should equal the balance for the current period's Accounts Payable Trial Balance.

For example, you are closing your accounting period for April and you have just posted your final invoice and payment batches to your general ledger system. To reconcile your accounts payable activity for April, make the following calculation:

April Accounts Payable Trial Balance = March Accounts Payable Trial Balance
+ April Posted Invoice Register
- April Posted Payment Register

120. **In Reports Payables Option, which of the following reports is not affected by this option Sort by Alternate Fields?**

   a. Accounting Entries Audit Report
   b. Cash Requirement Report
   c. Invoice Aging Report
   d. Accounts Payable Trial Balance

Answer: d

Explanation:

In Reports Payables Options, the following table lists the reports affected by this option Sort by Alternate Fields.

Report Name	Sorted by Supplier Name	Sorted by Supplier Site Name	Sorted by Bank Account Name
Accounting Entries Audit Report	Yes		
Cash Requirement Report	Yes		
Invoice Aging Report	Yes	Yes	
Invoice on Hold Report	Yes		
Invoice Register	Yes		
Preliminary/Final/Rejected Purged Listings	Yes		Yes
Supplier Mailing Labels	Yes	Yes	
Suppliers Paid Invoice History	Yes	Yes	
Suppliers Report	Yes	Yes	
Unaccounted Transactions Report	Yes		

121. **Which of the following navigation that leads you to open Subledger Journal Entry Lines?**

   a. Accounting>Subledger Accounting>Journal Entry Lines
   b. Setup>Accounting>Subledger Accounting>Journal Entry Lines
   c. Setup>Accounting>Journal Entry Lines
   d. Accounting>Journal Entry Lines

Answer: a

Explanation:

The correct navigation to open the Subledger Journal Entry Lines is Accounting>Subledger Accounting>Journal Entry Lines.

Illustration:

122. Which of the following navigation that leads you to open Accounting Events?

a.   Setup>Accounting>Subledger Accounting>Accounting Events
b.   Accounting>Subledger Accounting>Accounting Events
c.   Setup>Accounting>Accounting Events
d.   Accounting>Accounting Events

Answer: b

Explanation:

The correct navigation to open the Subledger Journal Entry Lines is Accounting>Subledger Accounting>Accounting Events.

Illustration:

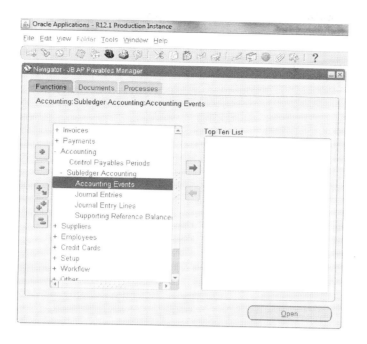

123. **Which of the following navigation that leads you to inquire payments Withheld Amounts?**

a. Setup>Payments>Inquiry>Withheld Amounts
b. Payments>Withheld Amounts
c. Payments>Entry>Withheld Amounts
d. Payments>Inquiry>Withheld Amounts

Answer: d

Explanation:

The correct navigation to open the Withheld Amounts Inquiry is Payments>Inquiry>Withheld Amounts

Illustration:

124. Which of the following navigation that leads you to inquire Invoice Overview?

a. Setup>Invoices>Inquiry>Invoice Overview
b. Invoices>Invoice Overview
c. Invoices>Entry>Invoice Overview
d. Invoices>Inquiry>Invoice Overview

Answer: d

Explanation:

The correct navigation to open the Invoice Overview Inquiry is Invoices>Inquiry>Invoice Overview.

Illustration:

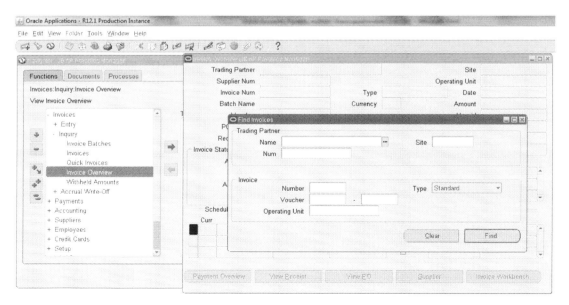

125. **Which of the following setup options is the correct navigation to enable or disable Allow Interest Invoices?**

   a. Setup>Options>Payable System Setup>Interest>Allow Interest Invoices
   b. Setup>Options>Financials Options>Interest>Allow Interest Invoices
   c. Setup>Options>Payables Options>Interest>Allow Interest Invoices
   d. Setup>Invoices>Options> Interest>Allow Interest Invoices

Answer: c

Explanation:

The correct navigation to enable and disable Allow Interest Invoices is Setup>Options>Payables Options>Interest>Allow Interest Invoices.

Illustration:

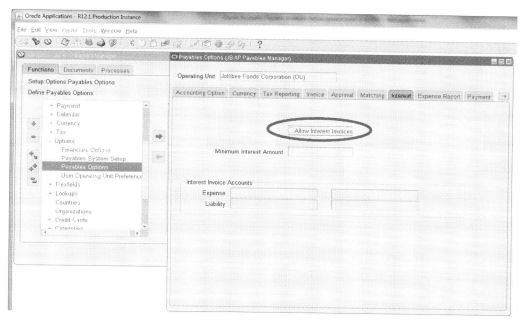

126. **In Invoice Workbench, what line types that captures the details of other charges on your invoices such as installation or services?**

   a. Item Lines
   b. Freight Lines
   c. Miscellaneous Lines
   d. Tax Lines

Answer: c

Explanation:

Invoice Line Information – Line Types

1) Item lines capture the details of the goods and services billed on your invoice.
2) Freight lines capture the details of your freight charges. Freight charges can be allocated to Item lines as required.
3) Miscellaneous lines capture the details of other charges on your invoices such as installation or service.

4) Tax lines - Payables integrates with Oracle E-Business Tax to automatically determine and calculate the applicable tax lines for your invoices.

127. **In Invoice Workbench, what line type that captures the details of the goods and services billed on your invoice?**

a. Item Lines
b. Freight Lines
c. Miscellaneous Lines
d. Tax Lines

Answer: a

Explanation:

Invoice Line Information – Line Types

1) Item lines capture the details of the goods and services billed on your invoice.
2) Freight lines capture the details of your freight charges. Freight charges can be allocated to Item lines as required.
3) Miscellaneous lines capture the details of other charges on your invoices such as installation or service.
4) Tax lines - Payables integrates with Oracle E-Business Tax to automatically determine and calculate the applicable tax lines for your invoices.

128. **In Entering Freight Distributions, which of the following does not belong to ways to create freight distributions?**

a. Enable the Automatically Create Freight Distribution Payables Option
b. Allocate freight across invoice distributions
c. Manually enter freight distributions
d. Automate Tax Distribution

Answer: d

Explanation:

There are three ways to create freight distributions:

1) Enable the Automatically Create Freight Distribution Payables Option
2) Allocate freight across invoice distributions
3) Manually enter freight distributions

129. **In Invoice Workbench, Hold, Due Date, Gross Amount and Priority are parameters for accomplishing?**

a. Holds
b. Scheduled Payments
c. View Payments
d. View Prepayment Application

Answer: b

Explanation:

Scheduled Payments fields or parameters:

1) Hold

2) Due Date
3) Gross Amount
4) Priority

Illustration:

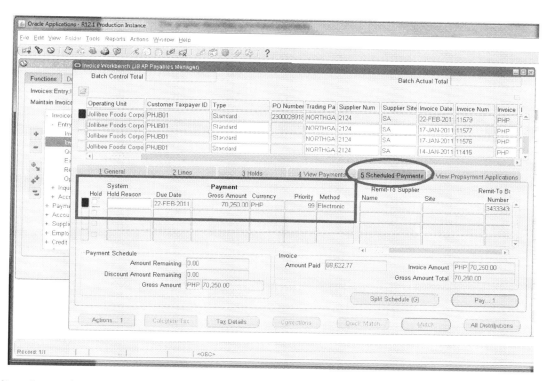

130. **If an item is used on the PO, the match approval level will default from the item and will override the supplier site. If the Item match approval level for the Item is match against Receipt required, then it result to what kind of match approval level option is this?**

a. 1-way match approval level
b. 2-way match approval level
c. 3-way match approval level
d. 4-way match approval level

Answer: c

Explanation:

If an item is used on the PO, the match approval level will default from the item and will override the supplier site. If the Item match approval level for the Item = Receipt required, then it results in a 3-way match.

131. **If an item is used on the PO, the match approval level will default from the item and will override the supplier site. If the Item match approval level for the Item is match against Inspection required, then it result to what kind of match approval level option is this?**

a. 1-way match approval level
b. 2-way match approval level
c. 3-way match approval level
d. 4-way match approval level

Answer: d

Explanation:

If an item is used on the PO, the match approval level will default from the item and will override the supplier site. If the Item match approval level for the Item = Inspection required, then it results in a 4-way match.

132. Which of the following is the correct navigation to enable and disable RFQ Only Site option?

a. Setup>Options>Supplier – Purchasing>RFQ Only Site
b. Setup>Options>Financials Options>Supplier – Purchasing>RFQ Only Site
c. Setup>Options>Payables System Setup>Supplier – Purchasing>RFQ Only Site
d. Setup>Options>Payables Options>Supplier – Purchasing>RFQ Only Site

Answer: b

Explanation:

The correct navigation to setup enable and disable mode of RFQ Only Site option is Setup>Options>Financials Options>Supplier – Purchasing>RFQ Only Site

Illustration:

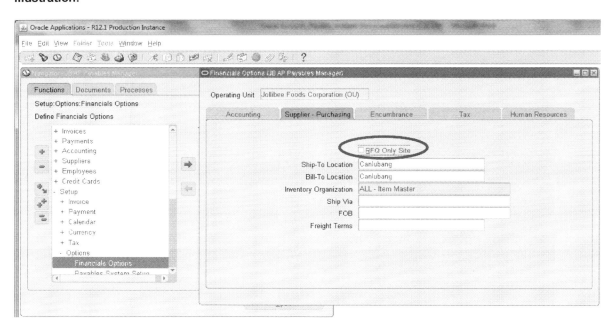

133. Which of the following is the correct navigation to enable and disable RFQ Only Site option?

a. Setup>Options>Supplier – Purchasing> Use PO Encumbrance
b. Setup>Options>Financials Options>Supplier – Purchasing> Use PO Encumbrance
c. Setup>Options>Financials Options>Encumbrance> Use PO Encumbrance
d. Setup>Options>Payables Options>Supplier – Purchasing>Use PO Encumbrance

Answer: c

Explanation:

The correct navigation to setup enable and disable mode of Use PO Encumbrance option is
Setup>Options>Financials Options>Encumbrance>Use PO Encumbrance

Illustration:

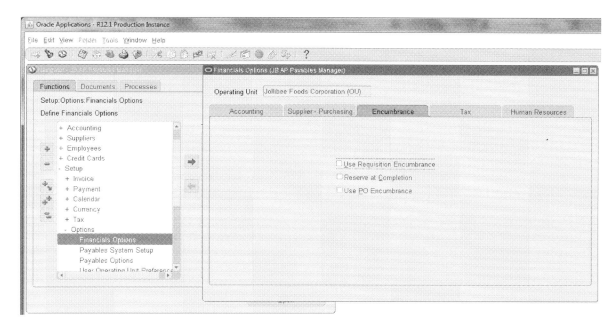

134. Which of the following is the correct navigation to enable and disable Hold Unmatched Invoices?

a. Setup>Options>Supplier – Purchasing> Hold Unmatched Invoices
b. Setup>Options>Payables System Setup>Hold Unmatched Invoices
c. Setup>Options>Financials Options>Hold Unmatched Invoices
d. Setup>Options>Payables Options>Supplier – Purchasing>Hold Unmatched Invoices

Answer: b

Explanation:

The correct navigation to setup enable and disable mode of Hold Unmatched Invoices option is
Setup>Options>Payables System Setup>Hold Unmatched Invoices.

Illustration:

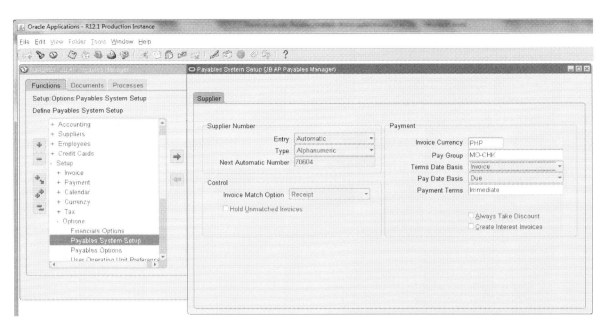

135. **Payable integrates with e-Commerce Gateway for exchanges of several EDI transactions. The e-Commerce Gateway can do the following except for?**

    a. Extract paid and closed invoices.
    b. Load invoices
    c. Load billing notices from an Advance Shipping and Billing Notice (ASBN)
    d. Create application devices to inform trading partners about events like duplicate invoices.

    Answer: a

    Explanation:

    Payable integrates with e-Commerce Gateway for exchanges of several EDI transactions. The e-Commerce Gateway can extract payments, load invoices, load billing notices from an Advance Shipping and Billing Notice (ASBN) and create application advices to inform trading partners about events like duplicate invoices.

136. **Run the Mass Additions Create program after payables invoice distributions have been transferred from Subledger Accounting to General Ledger (although the journals do not need to be posted). Which of the following invoice distributions criteria is not transferrable from Subledger Accounting to General Ledger?**

    a. Be transferred to General Ledger
    b. Have a clearing account associated with an asset category
    c. Have the track as asset flag unchecked
    d. Have a GL Date on or before the date you specify when running the process will be transferred to the FA_Mass_Additions table.

    Answer: c

    Explanation:

    Run the Mass Additions Create program after payables invoice distributions have been transferred from Subledger Accounting to General Ledger (although the journals do not need to be posted). To be transferred, invoice distributions must:

1) Be transferred to General Ledger
2) Have a clearing account associated with an asset category
3) Have the track as asset flag checked
4) Have a GL Date on or before the date you specify when running the process will be transferred to the FA_Mass_Additions table.

137. It is an interface table that holds Supplier information that is loaded by the user for import. The column of this table is mapped to the corresponding columns in the PO_VENDORS table. What do you call this interface table?

   a. AP_SUP_SITE_CONTACT_INT
   b. AP_SUPPLIER_SITES_INT
   c. AP_SUPPLIERS_INT
   d. AP_INVOICES_INTERFACE.

   Answer: c

   Explanation:

   AP_SUPPLIERS_INT holds Supplier information that is loaded by the user for import. The columns in the table map to the corresponding columns in the PO_VENDORS table. Payables uses this information to create a new Supplier record when the Supplier Open Interface Import program is submitted.

   AP_SUPPLIER_SITES_INT holds Supplier Site information that is loaded by the user for import. The columns in the table map to corresponding columns in the PO_VENDOR_SITES_ALL table.

   AP_SUP_SITE_CONTACT_INT holds Supplier Site Contact data that is loaded by the user for import. The columns in the table map to corresponding columns in the PO_VENDOR_CONTACTS table.

   AP_INVOICES_INTERFACE is a Payable open interface tables.

138. It is an interface table that holds Supplier Site information that is loaded by the user for import. The column of this table is mapped to the corresponding columns in the PO_VENDOR_CONTACTS table. What do you call this interface table?

   a. AP_SUP_SITE_CONTACT_INT
   b. AP_SUPPLIER_SITES_INT
   c. AP_SUPPLIERS_INT
   d. AP_INVOICES_INTERFACE.

   Answer: b

   Explanation:

   AP_SUPPLIER_SITES_INT holds Supplier Site information that is loaded by the user for import. The columns in the table map to corresponding columns in the PO_VENDOR_SITES_ALL table.

   AP_SUPPLIERS_INT holds Supplier information that is loaded by the user for import. The columns in the table map to the corresponding columns in the PO_VENDORS table. Payables uses this information to create a new Supplier record when the Supplier Open Interface Import program is submitted.

   AP_SUP_SITE_CONTACT_INT holds Supplier Site Contact data that is loaded by the user for import. The columns in the table map to corresponding columns in the PO_VENDOR_CONTACTS table.

   AP_INVOICES_INTERFACE is a Payable open interface tables.

139.Which of the following is the correct navigation to setup Invoice Distribution Sets?

a. Setup>Options>Distribution Sets
b. Setup>Options>Payables System Setup>Distribution Sets
c. Setup>Payment>Distribution Sets
d. Setup>Invoice>Distribution Sets

Answer: d

Explanation:

The correct navigation to setup Distribution Sets is Setup>Invoice>Distribution Sets.

Illustration:

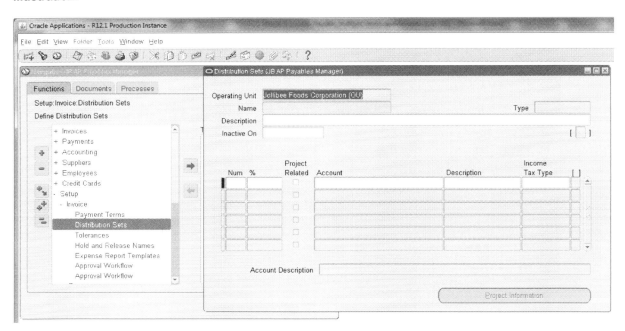

140.Which of the following is the correct navigation to setup Payment Administrator?

a. Setup>Payment>Payment Administrator
b. Setup>Options>Payable Options>Payment Administrator
c. Setup>Payment Administrator
d. Setup>Invoice>Payment Administrator

Answer: a

Explanation:

The correct navigation to setup Payment Administrator is Setup>Payment>Payment Administrator.

Illustration:

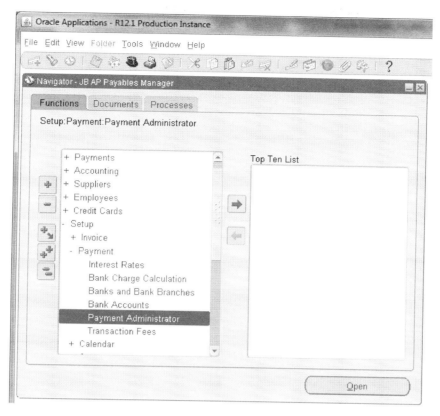

141.Which of the following is the correct navigation to setup Bank Accounts?

a.   Setup>Payment>Bank Accounts
b.   Setup>Options>Payable Options>Bank Accounts
c.   Setup>Bank>Bank Accounts
d.   Setup>Invoice>Bank Accounts

Answer: a

Explanation:

The correct navigation to setup Bank Accounts is Setup>Payment>Bank Accounts.

Illustration:

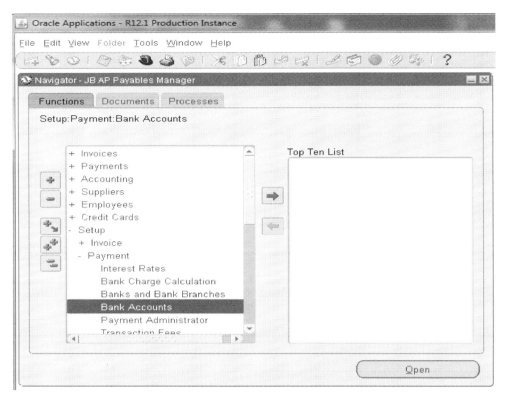

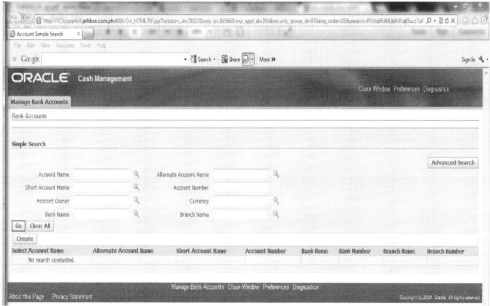

142.Which of the following is the correct navigation to setup Tax Reporting Entities?

a. Setup>Tax>Withholding>Reporting Entities
b. Setup>Tax>Reporting Entities
c. Setup>Payment>Tax>Reporting Entities
d. Setup>Invoice>Tax>Reporting Entities

Answer: b

Explanation:

The correct navigation to setup Reporting Entities is Setup>Tax>Reporting Entities.

Illustration:

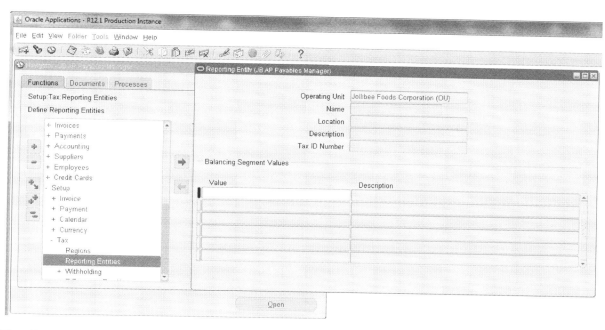

143. The 1099 Invoice Exceptions Report is divided into different sections. Which of the following is not a section of this report?

a. Invoice Distribution Lines for Non–1099 Suppliers with an Income Tax Type
b. 1099 Payment Report
c. 1099 Suppliers with a Negative Income Tax Type Total
d. 1099 Suppliers with Withholding Exceptions

Answer: b

Explanation:

The 1099 Invoice Exceptions Report is divided into the following sections:

1) Invoice Distribution Lines for 1099 Suppliers with No Income Tax Type
2) Invoice Distribution Lines for Non–1099 Suppliers with an Income Tax Type
3) Invoice Distribution Lines with Null or Invalid Income Tax Regions
4) 1099 Suppliers with a Negative Income Tax Type Total
5) 1099 Suppliers with Withholding Exceptions

1099 Payment Report is a separate report used to review payments made to 1099 reportable suppliers.

144. It is a report used to review paid invoice distributions with inaccurate or missing 1099 income tax information?

a. 1099 Invoice Exception Report
b. 1099 Payment Report
c. 1099 Electronic Media

d.   1099 Supplier Exceptions Report

Answer: a

Explanation:

1099 Invoice Exception Report is used to review paid invoice distributions with inaccurate or missing 1099 income tax information.

1099 Payments Report is used to review payments made to your 1099 reportable suppliers.

1099 Electronic Media is a report used to generate your summarized 1099 information in electronic format as required by the Internal Revenue Service.

1099 Supplier Exception Report is used to review suppliers with inaccurate or incomplete 1099 income tax information.

145. **It is a report used to generate your summarized 1099 information in electronic format as required by the Internal Revenue Service. What do you call this report?**

a.   1099 Invoice Exception Report
b.   1099 Payment Report
c.   1099 Electronic Media
d.   1099 Supplier Exceptions Report

Answer: c

Explanation:

1099 Electronic Media is a report used to generate your summarized 1099 information in electronic format as required by the Internal Revenue Service.

1099 Invoice Exception Report is used to review paid invoice distributions with inaccurate or missing 1099 income tax information.

1099 Payments Report is used to review payments made to your 1099 reportable suppliers.

1099 Supplier Exception Report is used to review suppliers with inaccurate or incomplete 1099 income tax information.

146. **Which of the following is the correct navigation for setting up a Withholding Tax Groups?**

a.   Setup>Tax>Groups
b.   Setup>Options>Tax>Withholding>Groups
c.   Setup>Tax>Withholding>Groups
d.   Setup>Options>Payment>Tax>Group

Answer: c

Explanation:

The correct navigation for setting-up a Withholding Tax Group is Setup>Tax>Withholding>Groups.

Illustration:

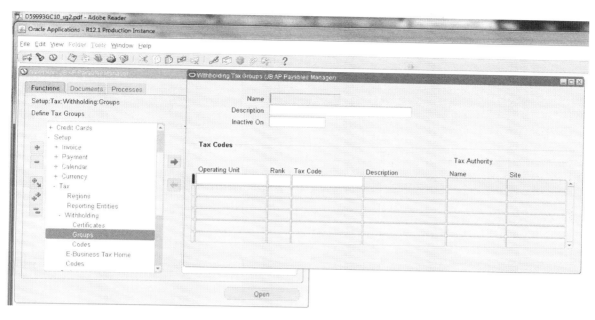

147. Which of the following is the correct navigation for setting up E-Business Tax Home?

a. Setup>Tax>E-Business Tax Home
b. Setup>Options>Tax>Withholding>E-Business Tax Home
c. Setup>Tax>Withholding>E-Business Tax Home
d. Setup>Options>Payment>E-Business Tax Home

Answer: c

Explanation:

The correct navigation for setting-up E-Business Tax Home is Setup>Tax>E-Business Tax Home.

Illustration:

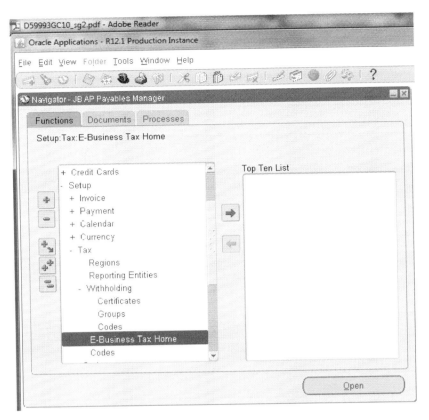

148.Which of the following is the correct navigation for setting up Tax Codes?

    a.   Setup>Codes
    b.   Setup>Options>Tax>Codes
    c.   Setup>Tax>Withholding>Codes
    d.   Setup>Tax>Codes

Answer: d

Explanation:

The correct navigation for setting-up Tax Codes is Setup>Tax>Codes.

Illustration:

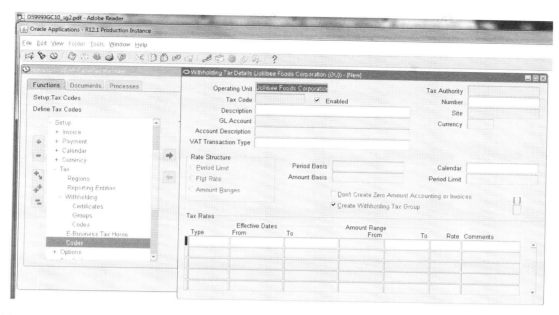

149.Which of the following is the correct navigation for setting up Tax Certificates?

a. Setup>Tax>Withholding>Certificates
b. Setup>Options>Tax>Certificates
c. Setup>Tax>Certificates
d. Setup>Certificates

Answer: a

Explanation:

The correct navigation for setting-up Tax Certificates is Setup>Tax>Withholding>Certificates.

Illustration:

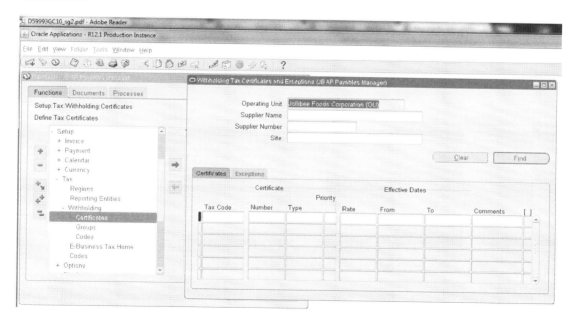

150. **Which of the following is the correct navigation to enable and disable Tax Combined Filing Program?**

   a. Setup>Tax>Withholding>Combined Filing Program
   b. Setup>Options>Tax>Combined Filing Program
   c. Setup>Options>Finance Options>Tax Reporting>Combined Filing Program
   d. Setup>Options>Payables Options>Tax Reporting>Combined Filing Program

Answer: d

Explanation:

The correct navigation to enable and disable Tax Combined Filing Program is Setup>Options>Payables Options>Tax Reporting>Combined Filing Program.

.**Illustration:**

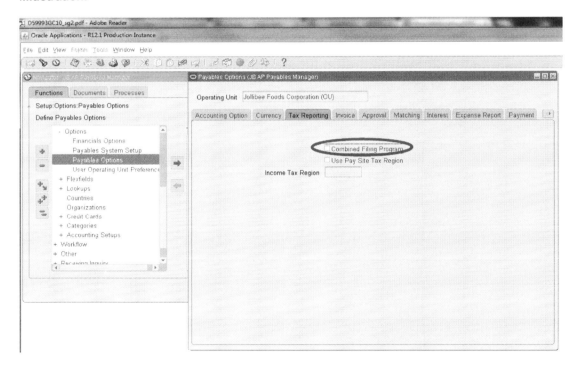

ORACLE E-Business Suite Essentials

1. This processing does not interfere with the interactive work you perform on your computer. This processing is also runs non-interactive tasks, such as reports and programs. What do you call this processing?

   a) Transaction Preprocessing
   b) Scheduled Processing
   c) Batch Processing
   d) Concurrent Processing

   Answer: d

   Explanation:

   Oracle E-Business Suite definition of Concurrent Processing is a processing does not interfere with the interactive work you perform on your computer. Concurrent processing runs non-interactive tasks, such as reports and programs.

   Illustration:

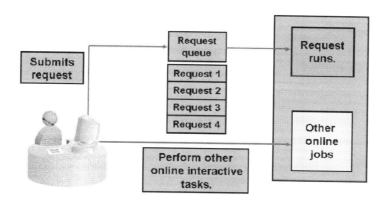

Using Concurrent Processing

2. Which of the following is an Oracle Order Management function?

   a) Oracle Inventory
   b) Oracle iProcurement

c) Orders, Returns
d) Oracle Order Management Super User

Answer: c

Explanation:

Oracle Inventory, Oracle iProcurement and Oracle Order Management Super User are Oracle responsibility while Orders, Returns is a function of Oracle Order Management.

3. **Using the Requests window (see below), what parameter was used?**

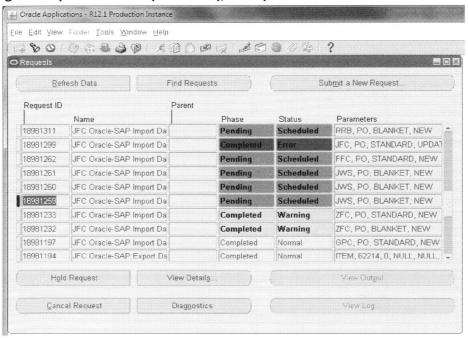

a) My Completed Requests
b) My Requests in Progress
c) All My Requests
d) Specific Requests

Answer: c

Explanation:

The parameter that was used was All My Requests. All My Requests parameter is use to display all concurrent request of a current user login.

Screenshot:

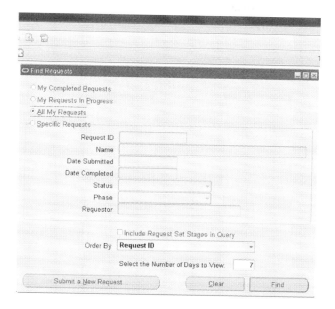

4. Using the Requests window below), what parameter was used?

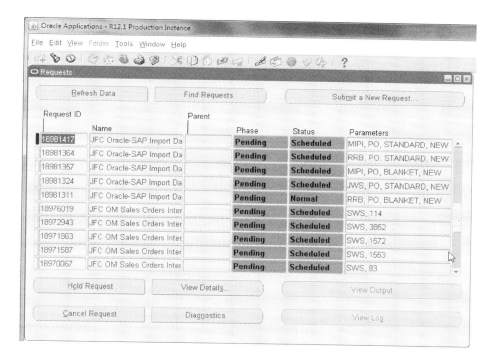

a) My Completed Requests
b) My Requests in Progress
c) All My Requests
d) Specific Requests

Answer: b

Explanation:

The parameter that was used is My Requests in Progress. My Requests in Progress parameter is use to display all concurrent requests at pending and running phase status of a current user login.

Screenshot:

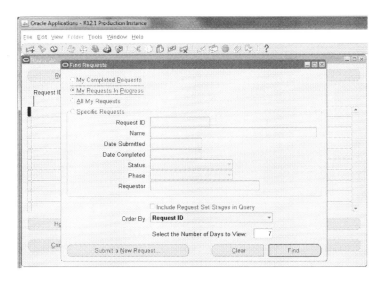

5. Using the Requests window below, what parameter was used?

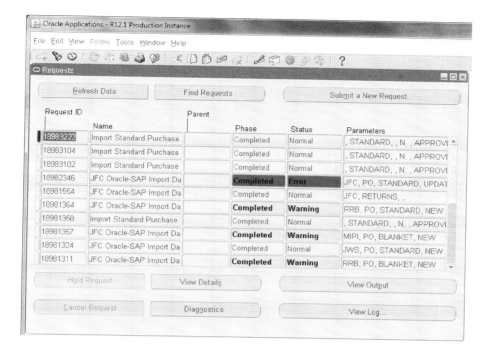

a) My Completed Requests
b) My Requests in Progress
c) All My Requests
d) Specific Requests

Answer: a

Explanation:

The parameter that was used is My Completed Requests. My Completed Requests parameter is use to display all concurrent requests at completed phase status of a current user login.

Screenshot:

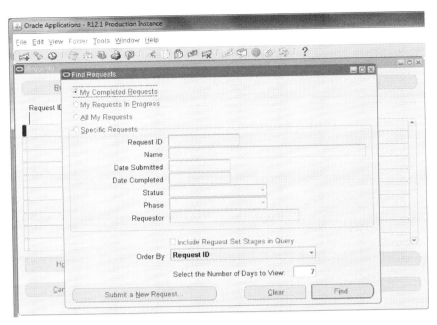

6. **This tier provides the user interface that could comprise desktop computers, laptops or mobile devices (such as PDAs). Its purpose is to capture and/or display information to the user. This basic technical architecture of Oracle Applications R12 is called?**

    a) Desktop/Client Tier
    b) Application Tier
    c) Database Tier
    d) Multi-tier

    Answer: a

    Explanation:

    Desktop/Client Tier provides the user interface that could comprise desktop computers, laptops or mobile devices (such as PDAs). Its purpose is to capture and/or display information to the user.

7. **This tier, sometimes referred to as the middle-tier, is responsible for holding the application logic that supports and managers the various Application components. This basic technical architecture of Oracle Applications R12 is called?**

    a) Desktop/Client Tier
    b) Application Tier
    c) Database Tier
    d) Multi-tier

    Answer: b

Explanation:

Application Tier, sometimes referred to as the middle-tier, is responsible for holding the application logic that supports and managers the various Application components.

8. **This tier supports and manages the Oracle database and is responsible for storing and retrieving application data. This basic technical architecture of Oracle Applications R12 is called?**

   a) Desktop/Client Tier
   b) Application Tier
   c) Database Tier
   d) Multi-tier

   Answer: c

   Explanation:

   Application Tier supports and manages the Oracle database and is responsible for storing and retrieving application data.

9. **Acts as the Web Server. It processes the requests received over the network from the desktop clients, and includes additional components such as Web Listener, Java Servlet Engine and JavaServer Pages (JSP). What do you call this server?**

   a) Oracle HTTP Server (Powered by Apache)
   b) Form Server
   c) Discoverer Server
   d) Report Server

   Answer: a

   Explanation:

   Oracle HTTP Server (powered by Apache) acts as the Web Server. It processes the requests received over the network from the desktop clients, and includes additional components such as Web Listener, Java Servlet Engine and JavaServer Pages (JSP).

10. **This hosts the Oracle Applications Forms and associated run-time engine that supports the professional interface. What do you call this server?**

   a) Oracle HTTP Server (Powered by Apache)
   b) Form Server
   c) Discoverer Server
   d) Report Server

Answer: b

Explanation:

The Form Server hosts the Oracle Applications Forms and associated run-time engine that supports the professional interface. This component of the Oracle Developer 6i, which mediates the communication between the desktop client and the Oracle database server, displaying client screens and initiating changes in the database according to user actions.

11. **This server is located on the node on which you maintain the data model and the data in your Oracle Applications Database. What do you call this server?**

    a) Oracle HTTP Server (Powered by Apache)
    b) Administration Server
    c) Discoverer Server
    d) Report Server

    Answer: b

    Explanation:

    Administration Server is located on the node on which you maintain the data model and the data in your Oracle Applications Database. You can carry out the following operations from this server:

    - Upgrading Oracle Application
    - Applying Database patches to Oracle Application
    - Maintaining Oracle Application Data

12. **An Oracle sophisticated tool that supports managing and monitoring of an Oracle Applications system from an HTML-based central control console. This is built into Oracle Application and complements the features of Oracle Enterprise Manager. What do you call this sophisticated tool?**

    a) Oracle HTTP Server (Powered by Apache)
    b) Oracle Enterprise Manager
    c) Oracle Discoverer Server
    d) Oracle Application Manager (AOM)

    Answer: d

    Explanation:

    Oracle Application Manager is a sophisticated tool that supports managing and monitoring of an Oracle Applications system from an HTML-based central control console. This is built into Oracle Application and complements the features of Oracle Enterprise Manager.

13. These entities in R12 E-Business Suite enable one-time definition of an object and the use of that object across several products. These are also "owned" by a single product for table purposes only. What do you call these entities?

    a) Oracle HTTP Server (Powered by Apache)
    b) Oracle Enterprise Manager
    c) Shared Entities
    d) Oracle Application Manager (AOM)

Answer: c

Explanation:

Shared Entities in R12 E-Business Suite enable one-time definition of an object and the use of that object across several products. These are also "owned" by a single product for table purposes only.

14. It provides Oracle EBS with a robust infrastructure for security, application administration and configuration. It also supports a mode in which a user account is automatically created for Single Sign-on (SSO) authenticated users when they first visit a page in Oracle EBS. What do you call this Oracle object?

    a) Oracle Servlet Library
    b) Oracle Application Object Library (AOL)
    c) Oracle Support Library
    d) Oracle Application Manager (AOM)

Answer: c

Explanation:

Oracle Application Object Library (AOL) provides Oracle EBS with a robust infrastructure for security, application administration and configuration. Oracle AOL supports a mode in which a user account is automatically created for Single Sign-on (SSO) authenticated users when they first visit a page in Oracle EBS.

15. It is an account structure that you define to fit the specific needs of your organization. You can choose the number of account segments as well as the length, name and order of each segment.

    a) Debit Account
    b) General Ledger
    c) Subsidiary Accounts

d) Chart of Accounts

Answer: d

Explanation:

Chart of Accounts is the account structure that you define to fit the specific needs of your organization. You can choose the number of account segments as well as the length, name and order of each segment.

16. **This information has three primary elements which are Chart of Accounts, Calendar and Currency. What do you call this data that provides the means to collect and quantify financial data?**

   a) Chart of Accounts
   b) Ledger
   c) Asset Accounts
   d) Expense of Accounts

Answer: b

Explanation:

Ledger is a data that provides the means to collect and quantify financial data. This information has three primary elements which are Chart of Accounts, Calendar and Currency.

Diagram:

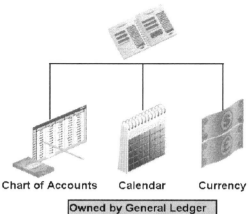

17. **This business flow outlines how a company uses sales order history to produce a forecast, design a production, manufacturing or distribution plan from that forecast and how to analyze. What do you call this business flow?**

    a) Demand to Build
    b) Order to Cash
    c) Procure to Pay
    d) Forecast to Plan

    Answer: d

    Explanation:

    Forecast to Plan is a business flow outlines how a company uses sales order history to produce a forecast, design a production, manufacturing or distribution plan from that forecast and how to analyze.

    Diagram:

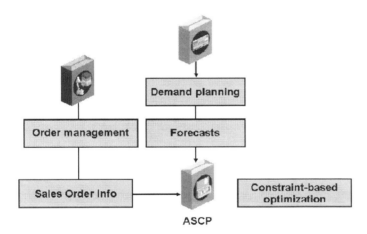

18. **This business flow outlines how a company creates purchase orders for procurement of goods or services, and then processes associated invoices for payment, transfer to General Ledger, and reconciliations with bank statements. What do you call this business flow?**

    a) Demand to Build
    b) Order to Cash
    c) Procure to Pay
    d) Forecast to Plan

    Answer: c

Explanation:

Procure to Pay is a business flow outlines how a company creates purchase orders for procurement of goods or services, and then processes associated invoices for payment, transfer to General Ledger, and reconciliations with bank statements.

Diagram:

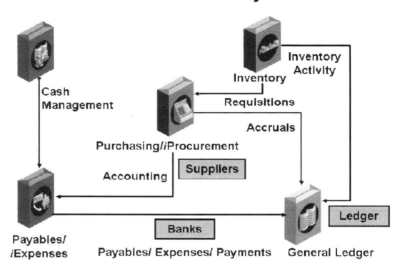

19. This business flow outlines how a company analyzes or anticipates demand and translates that demand into a production plan. What do you call this business flow?

    a) Demand to Build
    b) Order to Cash
    c) Procure to Pay
    d) Forecast to Plan

Answer: a

Explanation:

Demand to Build is a business flow outlines how a company analyzes or anticipates demand and translates that demand into a production plan.

Diagram:

Demand to Build

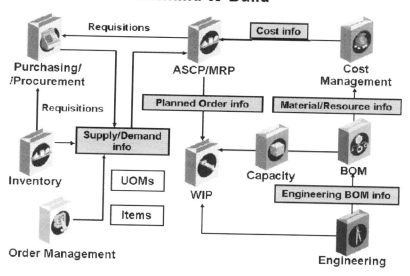

20. This business flow outlines how a company initiates, runs and tracks a market campaign to attract and secure more orders. This business flow in the slide does not reflect the complete back-end and integration with many of the shared entities, but depicts more of the front-end functionality. What do you call this business flow?

   a) Demand to Build
   b) Order to Cash
   c) Campaign to Order
   d) Forecast to Plan

   Answer: c

   Explanation:

   Campaign to Order is a business flow outlines how a company initiates, runs and tracks a market campaign to attract and secure more orders. This business flow in the slide does not reflect the complete back-end and integration with many of the shared entities, but depicts more of the front-end functionality.

   Diagram:

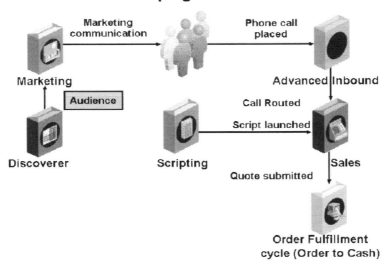

Campaign to Order

21. **This business flow relates to a company specifying its online sales setup. This flow encompasses activities starting from customer registration, setting up of products catalogs, setting up of targeted storefronts and finally capturing of the order. What do you call this business flow?**

   a) Demand to Build
   b) Click to Order
   c) Campaign to Order
   d) Forecast to Plan

Answer: b

Explanation:

Click to Order is a business flow relates to a company specifying its online sales setup. This flow encompasses activities starting from customer registration, setting up of products catalogs, setting up of targeted storefronts and finally capturing of the order.

Diagram:

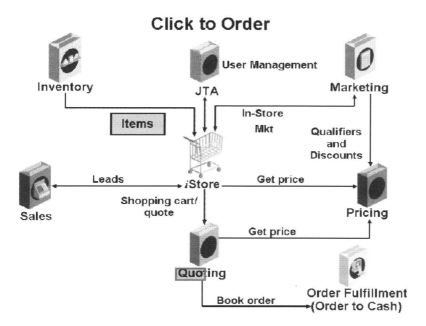

22. This business flow encompasses activities starting from order entry, checking/booking of the items in the inventory, shipping of goods, raising invoices, reconciling bank statements and transferring accounting entries to General Ledger. What do you call this business flow?

    a) Order to Cash
    b) Click to Order
    c) Campaign to Order
    d) Forecast to Plan

Answer: b

Explanation:

Order to Cash is a business flow encompasses activities starting from order entry, checking/booking of the items in the inventory, shipping of goods, raising invoices, reconciling bank statements and transferring accounting entries to General Ledger.

Diagram:

Order to Cash

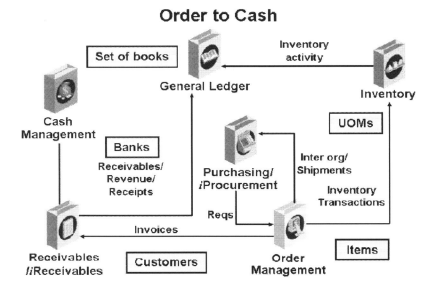

23. This business flow encompasses activities such as managing and renewing contracts (both manually and automatically), and authoring new service contracts for prospects or exiting customers. This business flow in the slide does not reflect the complete back-end integration with many of the shared entities. The modules displayed in the slides depict more of the front-end functionality. What do you call this business flow?

    a) Contact to Renewal
    b) Click to Order
    c) Campaign to Order
    d) Forecast to Plan

Answer: a

Explanation:

Contract to Renewal is a business flow encompasses activities such as managing and renewing contracts (both manually and automatically), and authoring new service contracts for prospects or exiting customers. This business flow in the slide does not reflect the complete back-end integration with many of the shared entities. The modules displayed in the slides depict more of the front-end functionality.

Diagram:

Contract to Renewal

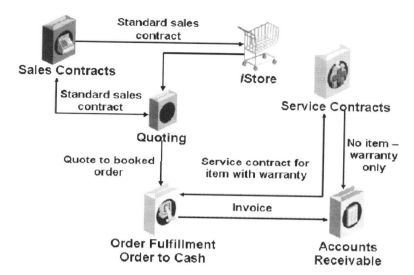

24. **This is a business procedure that enables a customer or customer service representative to create a service request, search for a solution from knowledge management, resolve and close that service request. This business flow enables companies to manage the service request lifecycle including service request escalation and charges for a service provided. What do you call this business flow?**

    a) Request to Resolution
    b) Click to Order
    c) Campaign to Order
    d) Forecast to Plan

    Answer: a

    Explanation:

    Request to Resolution is a business procedure that enables a customer or customer service representative to create a service request, search for a solution from knowledge management, resolve and close that service request. This business flow enables companies to manage the service request lifecycle including service request escalation and charges for a service provided.

    Diagram:

Request to Resolution

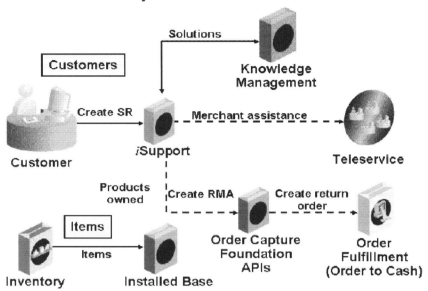

25. This business flow encompasses activities from project initiation, planning, scheduling and scoping. It also covers managing of resources and defines work breakdown structure and collection of expenses. What do you call this business flow?

    a) Request to Resolution
    b) Click to Order
    c) Project to Profit
    d) Forecast to Plan

Answer: c

Explanation:

Project to Profit is a business flow encompasses activities from project initiation, planning, scheduling and scoping. It also covers managing of resources and defines work breakdown structure and collection of expenses.

Diagram:

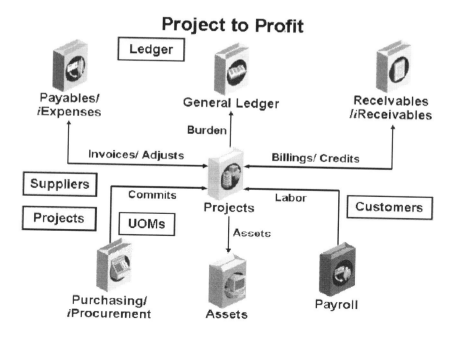

26. This business process encompasses activities related to calculation and generation of payroll payments to employees. This flow enables users to setup necessary payroll elements and methods for particular employees, perform payroll processing. What do you call this business flow?

    a) Request to Resolution
    b) People to Paycheck
    c) Project to Profit
    d) Forecast to Plan

Answer: b

Explanation:

People to Paycheck is a business process encompasses activities related to calculation and generation of payroll payments to employees. This flow enables users to setup necessary payroll elements and methods for particular employees, perform payroll processing.

Diagram:

People to Paycheck

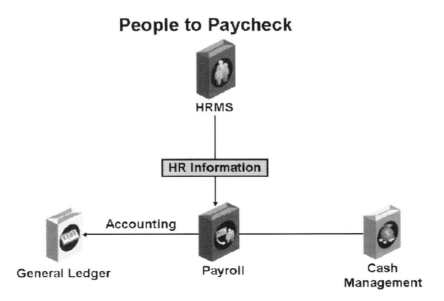

27. This restricts user access to individual menus of functions, such as forms, HTML pages, or widgets within an application. It allows you to define a user and assign the user one or more responsibilities within each responsibility having menu associated with it.

    a) Subinventory Assignment
    b) Function Security
    c) Organization Access
    d) User Responsibility

    Answer: b

    Explanation:

    Function Security restricts user access to individual menus of functions, such as forms, HTML pages, or widgets within an application. It allows you to define a user and assign the user one or more responsibilities within each responsibility having menu associated with it.

28. It is a collection of pairings of an application with an Oracle ID. These groups automatically support concurrent processing and cross-application reporting. These group guarantees that an application connects to a unique application database account. What do you call this collection of pairings?

    a) Request Group
    b) Item Category Group
    c) Data Groups
    d) User Groups

Answer: c

Explanation:

Data Group is a collection of pairings of an application with an Oracle ID. Data Groups automatically support concurrent processing and cross-application reporting. Data groups guarantee that an application connects to a unique application database.

29. **It is a list of concurrent programs that a responsibility can run. This group can include all the reports and concurrent programs that a user can run, individual concurrent requests, request sets and stage functions. What do you call this group?**

   a) Request Group
   b) Item Category Group
   c) Data Groups
   d) User Groups

Answer: a

Explanation:

Request Group is a list of concurrent programs that a responsibility can run. This group can include all the reports and concurrent programs that a user can run, individual concurrent requests, request sets and stage functions.

30. **Which of the following is not a step on defining a new application user?**

   a) Enter user name and password
   b) Require password change Limit Access attempts
   c) Enter User's start date
   d) Grant Role

Answer: d

Explanation:

Defining a new application user are:
   1. Enter user name and password
   2. Require password change Limit Access attempts
   3. Enter User's start date
   4. Assign one or more responsibilities

Grant Role is assigning a user a role to perform in Order Management.

31. **It is a set of executable code available as a menu option. What do you call this executable code?**

   a) Subinventory
   b) Responsibility
   c) Subfunction
   d) Function

Answer: d

Explanation:

Function is a set of executable code available as a menu option.

Reference:

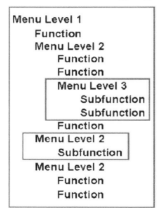

32. **Which of the following is not part of Profile Hierarchy Level of Security?**

   a) User Level
   b) Responsibility Level
   c) Application Level
   d) Location Level

Answer: d

Explanation:

Profile Hierarchy Levels of Security

1. User Level
2. Responsibility Level
3. Application Level
4. Site Level

Reference:

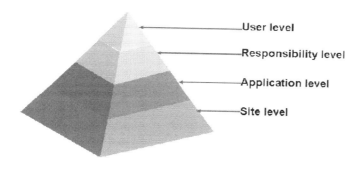

Profile Hierarchy Levels: Security

33. **It is a configurable field that opens in a window from a regular Oracle Application Window. When you define this, it enables you to tailor Oracle Application to your own business environment. What do you call this configurable field?**

    a) Numeric Field
    b) Flexfield
    c) Alphanumeric Field
    d) Field Trip

    Answer: b

    Explanation:

    Flexfield is a configurable field that opens in a window from a regular Oracle Application Window. When you define flexfield, it enables you to tailor Oracle Application to your own business environment.

34. **What type of flexfield that are used to define your own structure for many of the identifiers required by Oracle Application and drive reporting?**

    a) Key Flexfield
    b) Descriptive Flexfield
    c) Alphanumeric Field
    d) Character Field

Answer: a

Explanation:

Key flexfield are used to define your own structure for many of the identifiers required by Oracle Application and drive reporting.

35. **What type of flexfield that are used to gather additional information about your business entities beyond the information required by Oracle Application?**

   a) Key Flexfield
   b) Descriptive Flexfield
   c) Alphanumeric Field
   d) Character Field

   Answer: b

   Explanation:

   Descriptive Flexfields are used to gather additional information about your business entities beyond the information required by Oracle Application.

36. **It is a server-side (application and database) enhancement that enables multiple business units in an enterprise to use a single installation of Oracle Application products while keeping transaction data separate and secure.**

   a) Multi-Org
   b) Distributed setup
   c) Inter-Org
   d) Inter-company

   Answer: a

   Explanation:

   Multi-Org is a server-side (application and database) enhancement that enables multiple business units in an enterprise to use a single installation of Oracle Application products while keeping transaction data separate and secure.

37. **What entity that represents a legal company for which you prepare fiscal or tax reports? You assign tax identifiers or other information to these types of organizations.**

   a) Operating Unit
   b) Business Group

c) Organization
d) Legal Entity

Answer: d

Explanation:

Legal entity represents a legal company for which you prepare fiscal or tax reports. You assign tax identifiers or other legal entity information to these types of organizations.

38. **What do you call this accounting engine where it centralizes accounting for Oracle E-Business Suite products in R12? It is not a separate product in itself, but it is Oracle's engine catering to the accounting needs of Oracle Applications.**

a) Operating Unit
b) Business Group
c) Organization
d) Legal Entity

Answer: d

Explanation:

Subledger Accounting is mainly a rule-based accounting engine that centralizes accounting for Oracle E-Business Suite products in R12. Subledger Accounting is not a separate product in itself, but it is Oracle's engine catering to the accounting needs of Oracle Applications.

39. **It is an organization that can be used to model an autonomous business unit in an organization that has a business need to secure transaction data, set up and seed data. This unit can be set up to support different business policies and workflow process. What do you call this unit?**

a) Operating Unit
b) Business Group
c) Organization
d) Legal Entity

Answer: a

Explanation:

Operating Unit is an organization that can be used to model an autonomous business unit in an organization that has a business need to secure transaction data, set up and seed data. This unit can be set up to support different business policies and workflow process.

40. **This is an entity for which you prepare a balance sheet, represented as a balancing segment value in the accounting flexfield structure. What do you call this entity?**

    a) Operating Unit
    b) Balancing Entity
    c) Organization
    d) Legal Entity

    Answer: a

    Explanation:

    Balancing Entity is an entity for which you prepare a balance sheet, represented as a balancing segment value in the accounting flexfield structure.

41. **It represents an organization for which you track inventory transactions and balances.**

    a) Inventory Rack Location
    b) Inventory Location
    c) Subinventory
    d) Inventory Organization

    Answer: d

    Explanation:

    Inventory Organization represents an organization for which you track inventory transactions and balances. Examples are, manufacturing plants, Warehouses, Distribution Center and sales offices.

42. **Is an Oracle Application that automates and streamlines business processes contained within and between enterprises. What do you call this Oracle application?**

    a) Workflow
    b) Alert
    c) Security
    d) Process flow

    Answer: a

Explanation:

Workflow automates and streamlines business processes contained within and between enterprises.

43. **Which of the following processes that Workflow cannot be used?**

   a) Add personalized trading partner rules
   b) Validate self-service transactions
   c) Approve standard business documents
   d) Put physical product order quantity to 3PL truck.

   Answer: a

   Explanation:

   Examples where you can use workflow processes:

   1. Add personalized trading partner rules
   2. Validate self-service transactions
   3. Approve standard business documents
   4. Step through daily transaction flows
   5. Integrate with trading partners systems

44. **It provides a list of open notification for a particular user. It allows the user to view notification details.**

   a) Worklist Web Page
   b) Workflow Notification
   c) Error Notification
   d) Work Instruction Notification

   Answer: a

   Explanation:

   Worklist Web Page provides a list of open notification for a particular user. It allows the user to view notification details. It also allows the user to respond to notification that requires a response.

45. **Which of the following that Oracle Alert cannot do?**

   a) Send an email message
   b) Submit a concurrent program request
   c) Terminate a concurrent program request
   d) Run an Operating System Script

   Answer: c

   Explanation:

   Oracle Alerts can do:

   1. Send an email message
   2. Submit a concurrent program request
   3. Run a SQL Statement script
   4. Run an Operating System Script

46. **It is an integrated out-of-the-box reporting and analysis application that enables senior managers and executives to see relevant, accurate and timely information using self-service dashboards. What do you call this reporting and analysis application?**

   a) Daily Business Intelligence
   b) Datamart
   c) Data Warehouse
   d) Pivot table

   Answer: a

   Explanation:

   Daily Business Intelligence is an integrated out-of-the-box reporting and analysis application that enables senior managers and executives to see relevant, accurate and timely information using self-service dashboards.

47. **It is a set of new Application products and one of the first of the Fusion Applications. It works seamlessly with EBS 11i, R12 DBI and PeopleSoft EPM 9.0 Application and is part of the foundation of our Fusion Applications. What do you call this Application Products of Oracle?**

   a. Fusion Intelligence
   b. Oracle SOA
   c. Data Warehouse
   d. Pivot table

Answer: a

Explanation:

Fusion Intelligence is a set of new Application products and one of the first of the Fusion Applications. Fusion Intelligence works seamlessly with EBS 11i, R12 DBI and PeopleSoft EPM 9.0 Application and is part of the foundation of our Fusion Applications.

48. **It provides product cost and design information from the Oracle Product Lifecycle Management, Oracle Bills of Material, Oracle Engineering and Oracle Cost Management. What do you call this intelligence?**

    a. Fusion Intelligence
    b. Oracle SOA
    c. Product Intelligence
    d. Pivot table

Answer: b

Explanation:

Product Intelligence provides product cost and design information from the following products: Oracle Product Lifecycle Management, Oracle Bills of Material, Oracle Engineering and Oracle Cost Management.

49. **It Intelligence provides relevant, reliable, and up-to-the day data on the purchasing activities across an enterprise. What do you call this intelligence?**

    a. Fusion Intelligence
    b. Purchasing Intelligence
    c. Product Intelligence
    d. Pivot table

Answer: b

Explanation:

Purchasing Intelligence provides relevant, reliable, and up-to-the day data on the purchasing activities across an enterprise.

50. **It provides reports and KPIs to enable you to measure and analyze your supply chain. It provides information on the following management areas like customer, fulfillment, shipping, operations, plan and manufacturing. What do you call this intelligence?**

   a. Fusion Intelligence
   b. Purchasing Intelligence
   c. Supply Chain Intelligence
   d. Pivot table

   Answer: c

   Explanation:

   Supply Chain Intelligence provides reports and KPIs to enable you to measure and analyze your supply chain. It provides information on the following management areas like customer, fulfillment, shipping, operations, plan and manufacturing.

51. **It provides financial information to users in an enterprise, empowers the workforce, and assists them in making better decisions. What do you call this intelligence?**

   a. Fusion Intelligence
   b. Purchasing Intelligence
   c. Supply Chain Intelligence
   d. Financials Intelligence

   Answer: d

   Explanation:

   Financials Intelligence provides financial information to users in an enterprise, empowers the workforce, and assists them in making better decisions.

Made in the USA
Lexington, KY
12 November 2014